Get Over the Rainbow

Why *Everyone* Should Join the Fight for Gay Rights

By

Scott Redmond

authorHOUSE™

1663 LIBERTY DRIVE, SUITE 200
BLOOMINGTON, INDIANA 47403
(800) 839-8640
WWW.AUTHORHOUSE.COM

First published by AuthorHouse 02/10/05

ISBN: 1-4184-8218-8 (sc)

Printed in the United States of America
Bloomington, Indiana

This book is printed on acid-free paper.

Dedication

It is with honor that I dedicate this book to my fiancée **Brenda**
and my son **Sean** for their willingness to trade my attention for the
freedom to follow a passion.
To my beloved parents, **Ken** and **Diane**, who would never have
understood why their son would be the author of this book. I know
they are still with me and I'm sure they now understand.
And, finally, to **"Killer,"** my cat, who without fail curled up next to
the computer every night I wrote.

Table of Contents

The beginning of the rainbow....

On a frigid January Sunday afternoon I kicked the snow off my shoes and walked into a Denver bar that was crowded with Broncos fans watching the first playoff game of that season. Denver was buzzing with NFL playoff fever! About half of the patrons in the bar were wearing a Broncos shirt, jersey, or cap. Since it was a football game I was not surprised that the crowd in the bar was about 80 percent males and 20 percent females.

As I made the instinctive visual scan of the bar, assessing the surroundings, I saw a variety of drinks ranging from bottled beer to whiskey on the rocks. Since there was no law banning smoking in bars in Denver—not yet, anyway—the smell of cigarette smoke was thick. The Broncos were losing to the Colts and every time the Colts scored—which was often—the crowd let out an understandable moan of disgust. Even the women were revealing their knowledge of the game by second-guessing some of the plays called by the coach…and their observations were accurate!

That visual image would appear to describe any typical bar with typical football fans sitting around drinking and smoking while watching their favorite NFL team play on a Sunday afternoon. But in this bar on this Sunday afternoon, most Americans would not consider these patrons to be typical. In fact, many Americans actually *fear* that the patrons in this bar might, one day, be accepted as *typical*.

The bar scene I experienced on that cold January Sunday afternoon was at J.R.'s, one of Denver's popular gay bars. I can't be sure, but I had the feeling I was the only straight person in the bar. I was as comfortable there as I would have been in any straight bar. The reason for my comfort in that setting will be explained in Chapter 4.

The enthusiasm for a sporting event at J.R.'s was not unique to that particular gay bar on that Sunday afternoon. That was a familiar scene in gay bars all across America that day. Sitting at the bar, I was conscious that I was straight and everyone else was probably gay or lesbian. That led me to further contemplate the reasons for the deep chasm that currently divides homosexuals and heterosexuals in our society.

My heterosexual perspective yielded only one thing that differentiated me from the homosexuals in the bar. It was a difference that could not be determined from outward appearances. But the profound difference was a microcosm of the great division between heterosexuals and homosexuals.

The only characteristic that was responsible for what has been the age-old condemnation of homosexuality was the private act of sex. When the only actual difference between heterosexuals and homosexuals is defined by private sexual activity, it is impossible to logically justify any degree of discrimination by heterosexuals against gays and lesbians. And that's the premise of this book. Before I begin the straight argument in support of gay rights, including gay marriage, I want to first explain why the year 2004 was a significant year in the overall battle for gay rights.

The *newest* civil rights battle is underway

This decade might seem four years old, but in reality, it is just beginning. When the calendar turned to the year 2000, the monumental celebrations marking the historic moment of reaching the year 2000 and the perception of a new decade were several years premature. This decade did not actually begin until 2004. Looking back at the unique image each decade holds, it appears that the first three years of each decade continue to hold the images and trends of the previous decade.

This sets the stage for the evolution of the new trends that will define the decade. It is not until the fourth year of the decade when the unique image of the decade begins to be realized.

In the '60s, the battle for civil rights was fought over discrimination based on the color of a person's skin. The *newest* civil rights battle is being waged over discrimination based on private sexual activity. Should some people in America be denied certain rights because of personal sex? After the intense battle for civil rights in the '60s it is difficult to believe that we, as a society, once again must ask why a minority group is facing discrimination.

1964: the beginning of the '60s

Using history as a guide, the major issues and trends that will define any decade do not become obvious until the fourth year of that decade. In the 60s, the Civil Rights Act was signed in **1964**, the same year the Beatles arrived in America. In **1964**, the Cold War and the threat of nuclear war between the United States and the Soviet Union were a frightening reality for every American. Air raid drills at schools across the country manifested the daily fear that the Soviet Union could launch a nuclear missile that would destroy much of America. I'm still not sure why the schools thought that if we just got under our desks we would somehow escape the horror of a nuclear attack. A few people in the neighborhood I grew up in didn't ease my fears when they built bomb shelters in their backyards.

On March 26, **1964**, Defense Secretary Robert McNamara gave an address stating that the United States was determined to give South Vietnam increased military and economic support in its war against the Communist advancement from the north. That further solidified the U.S. commitment in Vietnam in the continuing fight to halt the spread of Communism. One of the primary reasons the United States did not fully unleash its military power against North Vietnam was the very real concern that the Soviet Union, which supported the North Vietnamese, would feel the need to enter the war to protect the North against U.S. support of the South. By treading cautiously in Vietnam, the United States was trying to prevent a worst-case scenario, which would have been a nuclear war breaking out between the United States and the Soviet Union.

Following the collapse of Communism in the mid-80s, and with it the end of the threat of nuclear war with the Soviet military, it has been tempting to second-guess the significance of U.S. involvement in a war in Southeast Asia. But in **1964**, the threat that Communism would spawn a web reaching our border with Mexico was quite real. Revisiting history and judging past events in the context of the current world is tempting, but flawed.

The passionate **anti-war protesting** of the Vietnam War, which would play a significant role in defining the '60s, began to reach a tipping point in **1964**, the year that would also be remembered for giving birth to the **anti-establishment rock generation** and the music, fashion, and pop culture it created.

Historically, the Beatles have mistakenly been credited with inspiring the youth rebellion of the 1960s, but the Beatles only happened to arrive in America at the right time. It was actually the assassination of President John F. Kennedy on November 22, 1963 that created a young generation's desire to dramatically reject the Establishment. The desire to reject the status quo of the Establishment is the responsibility of every young generation. However, each young generation subconsciously senses the need for the Establishment to provide a degree of security.

While an adult nation grieved over the death of President Kennedy, a young and innocent generation was shaken to its core. In 1963, parents did not always consider the impact tragic news events might have on their children. There should be no mistake about the reality that a young generation absorbed the magnitude of that national tragedy. Thus, an important sense of security had been suddenly lost.

The ever-present threat of the nation's destruction by **nuclear war** and the televised **murder of the President of the United States**, the presumed leader of the free world, caused an unparalleled loss of faith in the adult generation-the Establishment.

The Beatles landed on American soil in early February **1964**, less than three months after the Kennedy assassination. In search of anything that would distinguish them from their parent's generation, the young generation of the '60s embraced the unique sound and appearance introduced by the Beatles. The new trend represented by the Beatles was contrary to the collective taste and interest of the Establishment, which was precisely what made it so inviting to the non-conformist young generation of the '60s.

Grant it, the Beatles were only one of many groups that were part of a British invasion of music in the 1960s. However, the Beatles were the first to get national attention and have been singled out as the band responsible for the dramatic changes in young America in the '60s.

It has always been convenient to blame major changes in society on the more simplistic possibilities. The failure to understand the true reasons for the turbulence created by the original anti-establishment generation will only inhibit our collective ability to assess and predict more current social disturbances in our world. As we focus on 2004, it is important to recognize that the significant events of the 1960s reached critical mass in **1964**.

1974: the beginning of the '70s

On August 9, **1974**, Richard Nixon became the first president to resign the office of the presidency following the infamous Watergate scandal. March 18, **1974**, the OPEC oil embargo against the United States, Europe, and Japan ended. The disgrace **President Nixon** brought to the White House and the threat of a limited supply of oil in **1974** helped define the decade of the '70s.

The major events in 1973 set the stage for **1974** to become the defining year of the '70s. In 1973, U.S. involvement in the Vietnam War ended with the signing of a peace agreement. This brought an end to the war and an end to the divisive anti-war protests of the time.

In 1973, the U.S. Supreme Court ruled on *Roe v. Wade,* which legalized a woman's right to choose to have an abortion. When you consider the heated debate still inspired by the abortion issue, it doesn't take much imagination to envision the impact of the 1973 Supreme Court decision to legalize abortion in America. That decision by the high court reflected the rising status of women in American society. The idea that a woman could not be *forced* to continue a pregnancy demonstrated a liberating moment for all women in America.

The changing status of women leading up to, and after **1974,** was not without strong resistance from America's male-dominated society. On September 20, **1974**, the mostly symbolic tennis match between Bobby Riggs, a retired tennis pro, and Billie Jean King, a female tennis pro, was promoted as the Battle of the Sexes. Billie Jean King's victory over Bobby Riggs was more than a victory in an exhibition tennis match televised nationwide. It was a sign that women were actually rising to a level equal to men.

In **1974**, **the OPEC oil embargo** inspired the skyrocketing sales of smaller, fuel-efficient cars from Japan, thus leading to a complete overhaul of the American auto industry. As significant as it was, the OPEC oil embargo in the early '70s is dwarfed by current day concerns over the world's oil supply, which will lead to changes in this decade.

The resignation of Richard Nixon and the end of the **Vietnam War** began to define the political image of the decade. The **battle of the sexes** signaled the rising position of American women, which became a major debate by the mid-'70s.

Based on my recollection, there isn't much worth remembering about **music** and **fashion** from the '70s. Let's just admit from the mid-'70s into the early-'80s, **disco, polyester, head-banging metal rock,** and **the uniquely ugly hairstyles** that went with the music, including the *mullet,* are better forgotten.

Disco did get people dancing again in the '70s, but there was another constant music trend that dominated the '70s. It was hard rock best represented by groups like Led Zeppelin and Aerosmith. Regardless of the changing trends in music through the decades, hard rock and heavy metal have constantly attracted an audience that remains loyal today. And as it was in the '60s, the political and social events, issues, and trends that would define the '70s did not come into focus until **1974.**

1984: the beginning of the '80s

Politically, the '80s will always be remembered as the decade America took a hard turn to the conservative right. It was the re-election of Ronald Reagan in **1984** that solidified the conservative political and social trend of the '80s. By **1984**, tensions from the Cold War of the past began to fade, and later in the decade, the Soviet Union—the Evil Empire—would collapse, and with it, the threat of nuclear war and the fear that Communism would overcome Democracy in the world.

In **1984**, Madonna's *Like a Virgin,* Bon Jovi's *Bon Jovi,* and *Arena* by Duran Duran were some of the top albums that musically defined the '80s. Madonna made known her desire to create sexual and religious controversy with her music; Bon Jovi was typical of the big-hair, *cock-rock* trend in the '80s; and Duran Duran was one of the first *pretty* bands born on MTV. Groups like Duran Duran, Human League, and Men at Work represented the commercialization of punk rock that had been prominent in England in the late-'70s.

Original punk bands, like the Sex Pistols, were simply not marketable in America during the late-'70s and early-'80s. As a medium, music reflects its audience. Frustration over an extremely high unemployment among young Brits was reflected in the angry, aggressive tone of punk rock. America's youth did not share the same frustrations making the original punk sound too harsh for America's mainstream. However, by 1984 aspects of the punk sound had blended into the "new music" that would be unique to the '80s. The definitive musical genres of the decade became mainstream in **1984**.

The **re-election of Reagan** and the political turn to the right, **the end of Communism**, **controversy** over music and the new **"big-hair"** and **MTV bands** are the things that most of us remember about the '80s. All of those defining events and trends came to light in **1984**.

1994: the beginning of the '90s

In 1993, Bill Clinton became the first member of the Baby Boomer generation to become a resident of the White House. The popularity of Clinton's moderate political image seemed to indicate that America was rejecting the conservative right and turning toward the middle. Early in his presidential bid, Democratic candidate Bill Clinton also rejected the stricter liberal ideology that was so much a part of the Baby Boomer generation's earlier years. By the mid-'90s, moderate political views were dominant.

However, the conservative right did not go away without a fight. In **1994**, as a reaction to a Democrat becoming president, conservatives in America rallied behind the desire to steer the country back to the political right. Republicans won control of both houses of Congress for the first time in over forty years. But Speaker of the House Newt Gingrich (R) tainted the victory with his attitude. Gingrich acted like a kid who had just gotten the key to a candy store. Gingrich sent a clear message that conservatives were in control of America's political and moral direction, even though a Democrat was in the White House.

The Republican takeover of Congress was misinterpreted. By **1994** America was moderate. The more Gingrich gloated the more apparent it became that America was not going to return to the conservative ideology of the '80s. Speaker of the House Gingrich became a liability to the Republican Party and was replaced. Though he is still celebrated as a superstar in the Republican Party, it was Newt Gingrich's cocky attitude in '94 that almost immediately turned him into the "Gingrich that stole Congress."

It was in **1994** when Shannon Faulkner became the *first* female student admitted to The Citadel. On March 12, **1994**, the Church of England ordained its *first* female priest. These were definite signs that the Women's Lib Movement from the '70's had indeed elevated the position of women in America.

By **1994**, music had changed dramatically. The grunge-alternative music from Nirvana, Pearl Jam, and Soundgarden was adopted by the mainstream youth in America. The new sound, which was mainstream by **1994**, was the first major departure from decades of rock music that had been built on the rock music foundation first established by the Beatles and other British groups in the mid-'60s.

The new music of a new young generation inspired a drastic change in fashion not seen since the mid-'60s. The butt-tight jeans, the glitter, and the pretty bands born on MTV were replaced by baggy pants, flannel shirts, Doc Martins, shaved or dramatically colored hair, and a scruffy natural look. *Non-fashion* became fashion. This was clearly an attempt by a new young generation to definitively reject the status quo of the Establishment and become the *new* "anti-establishment" generation.

By **1994**, the music and fashion adopted by a new young generation signaled the most drastic youth rebellion since the mid-'60s. These were the children of the *original* anti-establishment generation. In **1994**, parents expressed the same criticism of the music and the fashion that *their* parents expressed in 1964!

Like it was in the '60s, '70s, and '80s, the '90s did not begin to be defined until **1994**. **Clinton** was well established as a moderate Baby Boomer president by **'94**. This was evidence the nation had turned away from the political and social right and extreme left. The progress of the **Women's Liberation Movement** was producing major changes for women in America by **1994,** and **the grunge rock music** and newly-inspired **fashion** of the '90s were the defining events and trends all beginning in **1994**.

2004: the 2000s begin!

At the close of 1999, I predicted on the talk radio show I was hosting in Portland, Oregon that gay rights would erupt as the major political/social issue of the decade. By 2004 that prediction had become reality. The political, social, music, and fashion trends that would define the decade were becoming obvious by 2004.

The re-election of George W. Bush in **2004** would seemingly send America back in time to the year 1984, when conservative ideology was dominant. Would another four years of a Bush administration reinforce the conservative tide that was rising? Conservatives have a tendency to dictate a moral path for America-a moral path subjectively based on conservative politics and religious beliefs.

The election of George W. Bush and the Republican gains in Congress may be interpreted as a mandate that America is once again craving the political and moral guidance of conservatives. But consider that the overall votes for Democrat John Kerry in **2004** were viewed more as votes *against* Bush than votes *for* Kerry. That means a very large percentage of Americans have demonstrated that there is *no* strong mandate for this country to return to the dominance of the conservative ideology from the '80's. It will be historically tempting to compare the **2004** Bush re-election to the 1984 re-election of Reagan. But history will show that the Bush victory was not a signal to reinforce the conservative politics of the '80s.

Four and a half years ago in Portland, Oregon I was doing a radio talk show with the idea that the overall available listening audience had become over-saturated with hard-core conservative talk radio. Four and a half years later radio experienced a new surge of liberal talk radio in the form of Air America, the radio network conceived by liberal comedian/author Al Franken.

Over that period of four and a half years I must honestly tell you that the program directors of the radio stations I worked for were not buying into the concept that the radio marketplace had become too heavily serviced by conservative talk shows.

Management at the radio station in Portland did not see the writing on the wall, even though it was *their* wall! In **2004** that radio station was directed by corporate leaders to syndicate Air America. After its first rating period in the market, Air America ranked #3 in the coveted 25-54 male demographic.

During the lead up to the war in Iraq, Clear Channel Communications, the largest owner of radio stations in America, was often accused of promoting the policies of the Bush administration because of close business ties to the Bush family. The fact that San Antonio, Texas was home to the corporate offices of Clear Channel further ignited the urban myth. I was with Clear Channel during that time and I can tell you that there was *never* a company agenda to dictate the opinions of talk show hosts. When the need for non-conservative talk radio was becoming reality prior to the election in **2004**, Clear Channel stations across the country began syndicating the Air America radio network.

Here's why there will be a difference between the re-election of Reagan in 1984 and the re-election of Bush in **2004**. The domination of conservative talk radio has caused many Americans to feel *their* voice has been completely shut out of talk radio. That frustration combined with the Bush "hate factor" has created a new environment for talk radio in America.

Conservative talk radio was born in the '80s as a result of the perceived liberal media ignoring the *conservative voice*. Liberal talk radio was born as a result of non-conservatives feeling *their* voice has been shut out of talk radio.

By the end of 2003, music was changing as it usually does by the fourth year of a decade. The "pretty-boy-dancing-bands" like the Backstreet Boys and N'SYNC were a memory. Bands that weren't "pretty" and didn't dance returned with simple lyrics and guitar-dominated music.

In **2004**, there was the resurrection of a musical genre reminiscent of the simplicity of the music of the '60s. Within the first eight months of **2004**, new groups like Maroon 5, The Killers and Keane best captured the new musical trend that would be remembered as the "sound of the 2000s."

Britney Spears and Christina Aguilera no longer represented the new trend that dominated the music scene in the early 2000s. Young male singers with unpolished, natural looks, like John Mayer, were also helping define the musical trend of this decade.

By **2004**, new fashion trends had begun to rise from the early adopters. What once was "geeky" had become fashion. The hippest members of the new young generation were going to secondhand stores to buy retro clothing from the '60s and '70s. The political, social, music, and fashion trends that would define the 2000s began to be realized in the fourth year of the decade-**2004**.

This brief journey through the recent decades illustrates that the celebration at the beginning of the year 2000 was mostly symbolic and not actually the celebration of a new decade. On the calendar a new decade appears to commence with the first year of the decade, but the political, social and pop culture trends that will ultimately define each decade do not become obvious until the fourth year. The political, social, music, and fashion trends that developed in the early 2000s set the stage for **2004** to follow the precedent set by history. As we all look back on the 2000s, we will see that **2004** was the beginning of the 2000s.

What the battle over gay marriage can teach us

The battle over gay marriage in America is history repeating itself. The past disagreements over the legal use of birth control pills and legal abortion were equally divisive. It was only through historic U.S. Supreme Court rulings that birth control pills were legalized in the '60s and abortion was legalized in the '70s. And it will be a U.S. Supreme Court ruling in this decade that will open the door for legal same-sex marriage in America. Those anxious to argue that legal gay marriage will *never* become a reality will only join those who made similar arguments against the legalization of birth control pills and abortion.

Recent court rulings on gay-oriented issues clearly demonstrate that our courts are on the threshold of ruling that same-sex marriage cannot be prohibited. This has made necessary the proposed constitutional amendments defining marriage as a union between a man and a woman only both on the state and national level. Chapter

1: **Gays go to court** uses past controversial issues to lend a view into the future of legal gay marriage.

This book addresses the various fear tactics being used by the Religious Right and many conservatives to predict the apocalyptic effect gay marriage would have on America.

The battle against gay marriage is being fought on a political and a religious front-often simultaneously. Chapter 3: **Does God love homosexuals, too?** presents rebuttals to the countless religious-based reasons to condemn gay marriage and homosexuality in the name of God.

In order to fully understand why homosexuality, in general, has become a heated and divisive issue in America it is imperative to have a fundamental understanding of the forces that shape the news and entertainment media. The digressions in this book are designed to provide such insight. You will learn that "Hollywood" is not pushing a "gay agenda" on America.

The fight to grant gays and lesbians the right to legal marriage will not be stopped by the saturation of conservative radio talk show hosts. Using Rush Limbaugh, the King of Conservative Talk Radio, as an example, Chapter 7: **Is right-wing radio killing gay rights?** explains why right-wing talk radio *does not* have the power to prevent the legalization of gay marriage.

The greatest pleasure I had in writing this book was the sense that it was the first cohesive account from the perspective of a heterosexual male of why gay rights, including gay marriage, must be supported. As a straight male I stood nothing to gain personally from legalizing gay marriage.

I also enjoyed discovering the reason I have always had a strong bond with the gay community. One need not be gay to feel such a bond. And then there is the love story between a lesbian and me, which led me to believe that every heterosexual should have a homosexual friend!

Read this book with an open mind and have the foresight to know that the issue of gay rights is not going away. A poll on May 18, 2004 showed that the backlash towards same-sex marriage was fading and support was growing. That poll was taken days *before* the state of Massachusetts began issuing marriage licenses to gay males and lesbians. That was an obvious indication that once gay marriage becomes part of the fabric of America and the gloomy predictions of our society's destruction are proven to be wrong, a majority of Americans will support gay marriage.

There is a generally accepted fear that gay marriage will hurt society and destroy marriage as an institution and a tradition. But it is heterosexuals, not homosexuals, who have disgraced and destroyed what was once a most sacred institution.

Anyone in America can fly to Las Vegas and get married within hours. Britney Spears married a guy from her hometown of Kentwood, Louisiana during an alcohol-induced adventure one night in Vegas. The marriage was annulled fifty-five hours later. And that is one of many examples of heterosexuals getting married without proper regard for the institution of marriage.

On May 17, 2004, America celebrated the fiftieth anniversary of the case of *Brown v. Board of Education.* That was the landmark Supreme Court decision that rocked the nation by ending the segregation of public schools. Fifty years later, we look back and wonder *why* there was ever a debate over granting black children the right to go to school with white children.

If you *support* legal gay marriage, this book will reinforce that support. It will also enhance your arguments as this new civil rights battle rages on. If you *oppose* gay marriage, you may come to the end of this book and look back and realize that the battle being waged to prohibit homosexuals from the right to legal marriage was wrong.

The right to gay marriage in America is motivated, in part, by the desire to feel more assimilated into society. Our past has taught us the *any* form of discrimination defies the spirit of America. I look forward to you reaching **the end of this rainbow.**

PART I

Chapter 1

Gays go to Court!

In the summer of 2003, the U.S. Supreme Court rocked America by ruling that laws banning "gay sex" were unconstitutional. Immediately there was widespread fear among many conservatives that declaring "gay sex" legal would lead to gay marriage. But long before the legality of gay sex or gay marriage became a major part of the social and political debates in America, the U.S. Supreme Court set the tone for future rulings that would favor homosexuals and lead many conservative Christians to predict the destruction of our society!

Ten years prior to the ruling that gay sex was protected by the Constitution, the U.S. Supreme Court made a significant ruling, which should have been a clear warning that the legal system was on the verge of changing its collective attitude towards gay rights.

In 1992, Colorado was nicknamed "The Hate State." Voters approved, 52 percent to 47 percent, Amendment 2, which forced the Colorado state constitution to repeal and prohibit *any* anti-discrimination ordinances passed by any municipality or any agency that would ban discrimination based on homosexual, lesbian, or bisexual orientation. In other words, a majority of voters in Colorado voted for the legal right to pass laws that would discrimination against homosexuals.

Below is the text of Colorado State Constitution Amendment 2:

No Protected Status Based on Homosexual, Lesbian, or Bisexual Orientation. Neither the State of Colorado, through any of its branches or departments, nor any of its agencies, political subdivisions, municipalities or school districts, shall enact, adopt or enforce any statute, regulation, ordinance or policy whereby homosexual, lesbian or bisexual orientation, conduct, practices or relationships shall constitute or otherwise be the basis of or entitle any person or class of persons to have or claim minority status, quota preferences, protected status or claim of discrimination. This section of the Constitution shall be in all respects self-executing.

The fundamental argument in support of Amendment 2 was based on the idea that giving **special** rights to homosexuals was inherently and morally wrong. The amendment clearly addressed a desire to halt any attempts to make discrimination against homosexuals illegal.

Passage of Amendment 2 by a majority of the voters in Colorado raised an important question: Does the majority have a right to pass legislation limiting the rights of a minority group? That is the same question that arises from the current battle over gay rights and gay marriage.

On May 19, 1996, the U.S. Supreme Court struck down Amendment 2. The court said that Amendment 2 violated the right of gay men and lesbians to equal protection under law and further said the amendment stripped gay people of rights granted everyone else. The decision was a decisive 6-3. That ruling established a precedent as to how the U.S. Supreme Court would rule on the issue of legal gay sex, which many fear is a prelude to gay marriage.

Justice Anthony Kennedy, writing for the majority, wrote, *"We must conclude that Amendment 2 classifies homosexuals not to further a proper legislative end, but to make them unequal to everyone else. This Colorado cannot do. A state cannot so deem a class of persons a stranger to its laws."*

Justice Kennedy went on to say the amendment *"identifies persons by a single trait and then denies them protections across the board."* Kennedy also referred to Justice Harlan admonishing the Supreme Court that the Constitution *"neither knows nor tolerates classes among citizens."* (*Plessy v. Ferguson* (1896))

In no uncertain terms, the Supreme Court defied those Americans who condemned homosexuals on religious grounds. Not satisfied with the premise that all individuals are entitled to follow the course of their own lives, the goal of the conservative right was to impose upon others the morals of the Religious Right.

Do "gay rights" amount to "special rights"? Justice Kennedy wrote, *"We find nothing special in the protections Amendment 2 withholds. These protections...constitute ordinary civil life in a free society."* This was a ruling that might be considered a Pearl Harbor-type attack on right-wing conservatives hoping the U.S. Supreme Court would support the morals of conservative Christians.

In his dissent, ultra-conservative Justice Scalia wrote, *"Amendment 2 is designed to prevent piecemeal deterioration of the sexual morality favored by a majority of Coloradoans, and is not only an appropriate means to that legitimate end, but a means that Americans have employed before."* Justice Scalia also pointed out that Amendment 2 was *"Colorado's reasonable effort to preserve traditional American moral values."*

That should have sent a cold chill up the spine of every American.

Should the majority of voters in any state have the right to establish the moral standards by which a law-abiding minority is to live? What if the same majority of voters disapproved of heterosexual couples watching pornographic movies? And I'm sure many do. Would they have the right to prevent those heterosexual couples from enjoying adult entertainment in the privacy of their bedrooms? If the same majority of voters disapproved of heterosexual couples engaging in anal sex or oral sex, both of which fall under the category of sodomy, should they be given the power to dictate what sexual activity is appropriate for others?

The idea that a majority of voters, locally or nationally, should have the power to enforce their moral beliefs on others defies the basic foundation upon which America was built. Freedom of religion also means freedom *from* the religion of others.

Declaring Amendment 2 unconstitutional was a legal declaration that the majority does *not* have the right to dictate the behavior of a minority group. Majority rule is a fundamental concept in America; however, the majority cannot use its collective opinions to dictate the moral behavior of a minority. The legal rejection of Amendment 2 was a significant shift for the U.S. Supreme Court, which only ten years earlier had ruled *in favor* of Georgia's sodomy laws on the grounds of the *"moral disapproval of homosexuality."* That ruling essentially meant that the morality of the majority could be used to establish a moral path for a minority group.

Is "sex" protected by the Constitution?

The right to sexual privacy reaches the foundation of the issue of gay rights and gay marriage. The U.S. Supreme Court's ruling on birth control is one of the legal precedents that could be used to establish legal gay marriage in America.

In 1965, the U.S. Supreme Court recognized an individual's right to privacy by striking down a criminal statute that prohibited birth control in the case of *Griswold v. Connecticut.* However, the court did not specifically address the issue of the right to **sexual** privacy.

Legalizing the use of condoms and birth control pills opened the door to an increase in sex for the sole purpose of sensual gratification. In 1965 attitudes towards sex were quite different and *Griswold v. Connecticut* proved to be a very controversial court ruling that was strongly opposed by many Americans.

Birth control pills and condoms were sexually liberating. In the mid-'60s, pregnancy was the most significant manifestation of frequent sex. Sexually transmitted diseases were a concern, but in the mid-'60s STD's were easily remedied. The idea of having sex freely without the fear of pregnancy suggested the beginning of a more sexually permissive society. When pregnancy was the only serious consequence of having sex, birth control allowed for the immediate separation of sex for *fun* from sex for *procreation*.

In the case of *Griswold v. Connecticut*, the U.S. Supreme Court ruled that an individual had a constitutional right to privacy in making the decision of whether or not to conceive a child. That ruling struck down state laws that prohibited married couples from using artificial birth control. And it wasn't until the case of *Eisenstadt v. Baird (1972)* that the U.S. Supreme Court granted unmarried couples the right to contraception.

Ultra-conservative judge Robert Bork reviewed the case of *Griswold v. Connecticut* and in his opinion the Supreme Court mistakenly interpreted the Constitution. Bork wrote that specific language granting the right to privacy did not exist in the Constitution; therefore Americans do not have a general right to privacy. And to think that if Robert Bork had not smoked pot in his younger years he would probably have become a Supreme Court Justice! Oh, the humanity!

The right to privacy is the fundamental question in the debate over gay marriage. In the case of *Roe v. Wade (1973)*, the U.S. Supreme Court's decision to legalize abortion was based on the right to privacy. The court ruled that the Constitution did protect a woman's right to choose to have an abortion because of the right to privacy.

In June of 2003, the Supreme Court's decision in *Lawrence v. Texas* overturned the Texas sodomy laws, establishing a legal, not an emotional precedent, that sexual privacy was a fundamental right in America. That recent ruling shocked those who were opposed to adult homosexuals having the right to engage in sex!

The Texas case, which was a blow (couldn't resist!) to sodomy laws, revolved around two gay men who were having gay sex in their home. It has always been said that sodomy laws are ridiculous because of the unlikely possibility of gays or lesbians who are having sex at home actually getting caught by police. Well, it turns out that the next-door neighbor of the two gay men was so opposed to homosexuality that he reported them to the police!

What must the "911 call" have sounded like?
"Hello, 911?I'd like to report two men having gay sex."
"Sir, are they having sex in public?"
"No, they are having gay sex in their home."
"Sir, what are you doing peaking into their home?"

The U.S. Supreme Court allowed a lower court ruling to stand, essentially declaring the Texas sodomy law unconstitutional. There was an immediate uproar heard from conservatives and the Religious Right.

While the court's ruling in *Griswold v. Connecticut* did not establish Constitutional protection of sexual privacy, the 2003 ruling in the case of *Lawrence v. Texas* declared that sexual privacy was protected by the Constitution. This was a major step in the direction of legal same-sex marriage. How the U.S. Supreme Court interpreted the Constitution in 1965 was different from the court's interpretation in 2003. Traditions are often lost when the Constitution is interpreted to reflect the social and political ambiance of each era.

Fast and furious was the outrage from the conservative right over the U.S. Supreme Court's ruling that gay sex was protected by the Constitution. Shortly after that historic ruling, the Massachusetts Supreme Court ruled that gay marriage was protected by their state's constitution. Gary Bauer from the group **American Values** said that the Massachusetts Supreme Court should be ashamed of itself for undermining 2,000 years of an accepted tradition. **Focus on the Family,** another Christian Right group, denounced the ruling as another step forward on the path to immorality. (Chapter 3 explores questions about religion and homosexuality.)

Do homosexuals have the *right to choose*?
"What if…"

What if there is never any scientific evidence proving that homosexuality is genetic? ***What if*** everyone who is homosexual actually did consciously choose his or her sexual orientation? Even with a lack of definitive evidence that homosexuality is genetic, it seems obvious that homosexuals were born with their sexual preference. But for the sake of argument, let's ***pretend*** that homosexuality is a **choice**. Why would the right to choose one's sexual preference not be protected by the Constitution?

As a straight male, the government and those in my community have had no control over the partners I have selected to have sex with, date, or marry. Maybe if there had been *some* government intervention I would not have been married and divorced twice! No heterosexual would tolerate the government having control over the choice of a sex partner or a spouse. So why is there such widespread support for government intervention when it comes to that decision for homosexuals?

The historic U.S. Supreme Court ruling in the case of *Roe v. Wade* in 1973 was based on a woman's right to privacy. Anti-abortion Christians believe that abortion is the murder of a child. Much to the disappointment of the anti-abortion activists, the medical community has never defined the fetus in the early stages of pregnancy as a "child." If the fetus in early pregnancy were medically defined as a child, then abortion would not be legal today.

From a medical and legal perspective an abortion is the removal of tissue from a womb. There are no legal or medical grounds upon which to argue that abortion is legally murder, yet that reality does not deter the fanatical beliefs of anti-abortion activists.

Those who oppose legal abortion are generally the same people who oppose homosexuality. Let's give them credit for being consistent, but the law must be consistent, too. The Supreme Court ruling that established legalized abortion in America set a strong legal precedent on the issue of right to privacy. The selective process of recognizing an individual's right to privacy in one situation but not another situation is contrary to the intentions of our legal system. Right to privacy cannot be used to protect one action without protecting other equivalent actions.

The frantic anti-gay marriage activists will argue that those who *choose* to murder, rape, or rob, could use the right to privacy rulings to defend their actions. After all, that is a decision made within the boundaries of the privacy of one's own personal life. But the difference should be obvious. Murder, rape, and robbery hurt other innocent individuals. Homosexuality is a lifestyle, which has no victims.

Inane arguments have been made to the contrary, but actions between two consenting adults yield no victims. And as far as the argument that families are destroyed by homosexuality, I suggest that any individual's decision to violate the commitment of marriage is not related to homosexuality. There are countless more incidents indicting *heterosexual* sex for the destruction of marriages than homosexual sex.

Though I don't believe homosexuality is a choice, even if it were, the arguments in support of choosing to be homosexual are quite sound. A person's actions in the privacy of his or her life should be of no concern to others. Opposition to gay sex and gay marriage is an obvious attempt by the conservative right, and even many Democrats, to force their moral and religious beliefs on others.

The only thing that differentiates homosexuals from heterosexuals is physical sex. Opposition to the homosexual lifestyle invites the idea that the government should control *all* sexual activity that occurs in private. Legally, that would include the sexual activity of every heterosexual as well as every homosexual. Do you think Christian right conservatives want the government to control what happens in their bedrooms? Asking the government to pass legislation, which opposes gay marriage is an open invitation for the government to determine what private sexual activity is appropriate, whether heterosexual or homosexual in nature.

Heterosexuals enjoy oral and anal sex. There is no actual difference between heterosexual couples and homosexual couples participating in oral or anal sex. The actions involve two human beings performing the same sexual acts. Our legal system would be severely damaged if legal principles were applied in one case, but not another. Anal and oral sex are acts of sodomy; yet there is a grand misconception that only oral and anal sex with a member of the *same* gender constitutes sodomy.

And what of the many heterosexual women who enjoy engaging in sex with other heterosexual women? By its nature, that is homosexual sex, but does not carry the stigma associated with "homosexual sex." This further demonstrates that opposition to gay sex is based on the disapproval of homosexuality in general. Truth be known, many Christians participate in the same sexual activity they are so quick to condemn homosexuals for participating in with their partners.

To be...or not to be gay? That is the question!

If you are *heterosexual*, when did you make the *decision* to become heterosexual? If you are *homosexual*, when did you *choose* to become gay or lesbian? Were you eight, ten, twelve, fourteen, sixteen, eighteen, or did you *decide* to be straight or gay as an adult?

If you're honest you will admit that you never did make a conscious decision about your sexual orientation. If heterosexuals don't choose to be straight, then why can't it be understood that homosexuals don't choose to be gay or lesbian? There will always be exceptions to that, but those are **exceptions**.

As early as kindergarten I knew I was straight. To this day I have a vivid memory of Miss Linda, my kindergarten teacher, squatting down to tie my shoe. She did so in such a way that allowed me to look up her skirt and see her pink panties! I was a redheaded, freckle-faced kid in kindergarten! What was I doing looking up the kindergarten teacher's dress? At that moment, I only knew there was something *exciting* about seeing the teacher's pink panties. My first indication I was a heterosexual occurred in kindergarten. What does that tell you about our sexual instinct?

I was in kindergarten in the 1950s and at that time there were no concerns about children developing an unnatural and premature infatuation with sex as a result of the media. What led me to focus on Miss Linda's pink panties as I looked up her skirt was sexual instinct. It wasn't taught, it wasn't created by exposure to anything sexual. It was my innate sexual preference.

Another sexual incident occurred that same year. I got caught with the little girl next door in her garage. We had decided to show each other our privates! We were busted! I enjoyed seeing what I saw even though I didn't know why. I do remember that both of our fathers were not too happy! I was scolded but never regretted what I saw that day.

While it seems logical that sexual orientation is genetic, to date, there is no decisive research to support that widely believed premise. Even if sexual orientation can be traced to genetics through scientific research, the condemnation of homosexuals would continue.

Science Ministries Incorporated has adopted the position that even if homosexuality is scientifically proven to be genetic, the question of morality remains unanswered. Remember, the Religious Right is only interested in perpetrating the belief that homosexuality opposes God's wishes and it inherently wrong, rather than seeking the actual truth about homosexuality.

The crusade against homosexuals led by the Christian right is not guided by any desire to search for a truthful answer to the question of morality and homosexuality. The crusade has always been to condemn homosexuality at any cost.

Dr. Simon LeVay gained notoriety for his discovery that there is difference between the brains of heterosexuals and the brains of homosexuals. Dr. LeVay extensively studied the part of the human brain known as the **hypothalamus,** which is believed to control sexuality. In the brains of homosexual men, the hypothalamus was smaller. But this research does not prove that homosexuality is genetic and questions remained to be answered.

Is that part of the brain smaller as a distinction of homosexuality? Or did the chosen behavior of homosexuality actually cause that part of the brain to shrink?

The research conducted by Dr. LeVay yielded an important discovery, but it also provided ammunition for both anti-gay and pro-gay activists. Based on the research on the hypothalamus, anti-gay activists have argued that homosexuality is a *chosen* lifestyle, which could be the result of poor parenting, a lack of morality, or even the possibility that the behavior is Satan-driven. The pro-gay activists will continue to argue that homosexuality is not a chosen orientation, but is genetically determined from birth.

Richard Green, a psychiatrist at UCLA, tried to answer the question of whether homosexuality was genetic by comparing feminine boys with masculine boys. Assuming that femininity and masculinity could be genetic traits in boys, Green's goal was to interview boys when they were too young to understand enough about feminine and masculine behavior to choose one over the other. Following the same sets of boys over time, Dr. Green interviewed both groups of boys. The feminine boys and the masculine boys were interviewed when they reached their late teens and early twenties. Among the effeminate boys, 75 percent had become gay adult males. The concluding observation made by Dr. Green was that the effeminate boys were not *taught* to be gay. They were motivated by innate behavior, which was beyond their control.

From our early school years, we can all remember those male students who seemed to be different. They were more feminine than other boys were. They didn't seem to enjoy the same activities on the playground. But years ago, it was unheard of to conclude that any young boy was actually gay, or destined to be a gay adult. Those boys were referred to as "sissies" or "mama's boys," and maybe even "queer."

Today, a young person showing the characteristics of being a "sissy" would be described as being gay or homosexual. The research of Richard Green at UCLA does seem to establish a link between genetic behavior and homosexuality.

"Genes are hardware...the data of life's experiences are processed through the sexual software into the circuits of identity. I suspect the software is a mixture of both genes and environment, in much the same way the software of a computer is a mixture of what's installed at the factory and what's added by the user."

That analogy comes from Dean Hamer, who is known as the **"gay gene" researcher**. Through extensive research, Hamer concluded that genes only play a part in determining sexual orientation. Environment is the other determining part. That seems logical and is probably the case with many homosexuals. But it also seems logical to conclude that those males with the genes that determine homosexuality would be more prone to respond to an environment that would reinforce their sexual instincts. Or it could be a case of the environment adjusting to genetic-led behavior.

To date, there is no research establishing a direct link between genetics and sexual orientation. Sociologist Dr. Steven Goldberg wrote:

"Virtually all of the evidence argues against there being a determinative physiological causal factor and I know of no researcher who believes that such a determinative factor exists...such factors play a predisposing, not a determinative role...I know of no one in the field who argues that homosexuality can be explained without reference to environmental factors."

Many things in life cannot be proven by scientific research. The fact that there is no conclusive scientific evidence proving a genetic link to homosexuality is understandable.

There is no reason to dismiss the aspects of life that cannot be explained by scientific research. Would it be wrong to conclude that there is no link between intercourse and pregnancy, since some aspects of the creation of life remain a scientific mystery? Much is known about the process of creating life, but there is a leap of faith in accepting the results of sperm penetrating a female egg in the potential development of a human child. Does that make it any less acceptable? If homosexuality cannot be decisively proven by scientific research, then why should that mean it is less acceptable among other natural phenomena that cannot be scientifically explained?

The fact that homosexuality has yet to be genetically proven is welcomed by those who condemn the lifestyle. The reluctance to accept homosexuality as a natural lifestyle is based on the religious belief that homosexuality is a choice rather than a human instinct. For if it were proven that homosexuality was genetic the Christian right would find itself condemning God's creations.

The Christian right has used the American culture's repressed view of sex, in general, to fuel the crusade against homosexuality. There will always be a large percentage of people willing to openly denounce any sexual activity that is contrary to their fundamental view of sex. In the context of American culture, homosexual sex is considered deviant behavior by a majority of Americans. But choice of sexual activity should be a sacred aspect of the personal freedom we enjoy in America.

"There can be no truer test of personal freedom than sexual freedom because there can be nothing more personal or formative for the young adult than his or her own sexual expression," wrote Professor Thomas McNamara in his book, *Evolution, Culture, and Consciousness.* Professor McNamara concluded that the repression of our sexuality in Western culture has been inhibiting and has caused more emotional damage and *"waste of human potential than any other single aspect of egocentric consciousness."*

The sexual repression in our culture ranges from the failure to accept homosexuality to the criticism of a mother breastfeeding an infant in a public place. In recent years, states across the country have been required to pass legislation that legally allows a mother to breastfeed her baby in public. If, as a society, we must pass laws that make it legal for females to use their breasts in the manner in which God intended them to be used, we should not be surprised by any aspect of sexual repression in America.

Professor McNamara also writes:

> *"The only reason any progress has been made at all in the acceptance of homosexuality is because of the recent rebellion of the homosexual community against this cultural prejudice, following in the footsteps of the civil rights and women's movements. As an excellent example of egocentric consciousness, the traditional argument against homosexuality is based upon the cultural presupposition that all sexuality should be repressed unless it is directly contributing to basic evolutionary goals, such as social stability and genetic reproduction. Here again we see the underlying evolutionary principle that the needs of the reproductive group ought to come before the needs of the individual."*

Chapter Update:

As gay and lesbian couples began to receive legal marriage licenses from the state of Massachusetts on Monday, May 17, 2004, Governor Mitt Romney echoed the sentiment of many Americans when he was quoted in *USA Today* saying, *"An issue as fundamental to society as the definition of marriage should be decided by the people."*

In March 2004, the Massachusetts legislature passed a proposed constitutional amendment that accepted civil unions for same-sex couples, but not legal marriage. It would be some time before "the people" of the state of Massachusetts could voice their direct opinions on the issue of gay marriage. The legislature needs to approve the amendment again before the state can vote on the issue in November 2006.

Below is a list of the seven original couples that filed the lawsuit, which led to marriage licenses being issued to same-sex couples:

Chapter 2

Gay Marriage...the new social controversy

It's 2:04 p.m. on a beautiful, chilly Saturday afternoon in Denver, Colorado. The Election of 2004 has inspired pro-gay marriage protests. I have just returned to my computer after attending a gay and lesbian rally on the steps on the Denver City and County Building. There were at least 3,000 people at the rally. The rally was a show of support for gay marriage, as well as a public denouncement of President Bush and all of the politicians from Colorado who supported a constitutional amendment prohibiting gay marriage.

Denver Mayor John Hickenlooper, several members from the city council, and gay and lesbian activists all gave inspiring speeches, often interrupted by shouts and applause. But I was most interested in the crowd itself. Audience members always reflect the event to which they attend. Who were these people who would take time on a beautiful Saturday afternoon to go out of their way simply to show support for gay marriage?

I saw families. I saw children with same-sex couples. I saw young people and a lot of twenty-thirty-forty-fifty-somethings and a few seniors, too. There were African Americans, Asians, Hispanics, and whites. I'm sure I missed a few.

At the pro-gay marriage rally, I saw anger, frustration, and victimization on the faces of the individuals in the crowd. This revealed a focused, determined, and united force. At that point, it was obvious, though unbeknownst to many, this country was on the verge of a new civil rights battle. This crowd appeared so strong-willed that I knew their cause would advance.

One of the gay activist speakers talked about President Bush's criticism of "activist judges" who seemed intent on defying the majority and rewriting the laws in America. The speaker said she *appreciated* activist judges, like the activist judges who finally gave women the right to vote. She went on to mention the activist judges who forced America to begin treating blacks as equal citizens, and the activist judges who ruled the Constitution did not have wording to prohibit interracial marriages. And it was the activist judges currently on the bench who found laws prohibiting gay sex to be unconstitutional.

If activist judges did not interpret the Constitution in ways that defy the collective opinion of a majority of Americans, women *would not* be allowed to vote, blacks *would not* be treated as equal citizens, blacks and whites *would not* be allowed to marry, and consenting adults of the same sex *would not* be allowed to engage in sexual relations. America needs activist judges to protect the rights of individuals when a majority of the population resists a change that would grant equal rights to a minority group.

After the U.S. Supreme Court ruling which declared the Texas sodomy law unconstitutional in the summer of 2003, President Bush said he supported gay rights, but not gay marriage. California Governor Arnold Schwarzenegger, a liberal conservative who is pro-choice, had just been sworn in as the new governor of California. Arnie said he too supported gay rights, but not gay marriage. This is a slick attempt to appear sensitive to the civil rights of a minority group while simultaneously discriminating against them.

Do you recall the presidential election of 1992? Abortion was a big issue that year for the Republicans. During the campaign, a reporter asked President George Bush (Sr.) if he supported a woman's right to choose. His reply was "no." Then the reporter asked if he would oppose a family member having an abortion. Bush admitted he would allow the family member to make that decision. Vice President Dan Quayle was asked the same set of questions. Quayle said he was against abortion, but would leave the decision of abortion up to his daughter, for example, should she face an unexpected pregnancy.

Bush and Quayle were actually pro-choice even if they didn't realize it. By answering the question about abortion, both politicians demonstrated that in the case of a family member, the decision about abortion was to be left to the woman. Every abortion is the decision of someone's daughter, sister, or mother. If the president and the vice president would recognize a family member's right to make a decision about abortion, then they were **pro-choice.** But for political reasons, neither Bush nor Quayle could admit they were pro-choice.

The American voting public should do a better job of holding politicians accountable for their inconsistencies. But the voting public only hears what it **wants** to hear, rather than what is **actually** said by politicians. The conservatives who supported President Bush and Vice President Quayle's opposition to abortion only heard the part where they said they opposed legalized abortion. They didn't pay attention to Bush and Quayle's support a pro-choice stance in the case of family members.

America has treated the issue of gay marriage similar to the way it treated the abortion issue. So, let's make gay marriage personal. Vice President Dick Cheney's daughter is a lesbian. Though publicly opposing gay marriage for political reasons, it would take a father who lacked compassion not to support his daughter's right to marry her partner. Well, the fact that the "father" in this case is Dick Cheney, his daughter might *not* get his personal support!

In November 2003, a major ruling by the Massachusetts Supreme Court caused a new uproar over gay rights. The Massachusetts Supreme Court ruled, by a 4-3 vote, that the state's constitution contained no specific wording that prohibited same-sex marriage. This was the first time a court had decided that even though same-sex marriage was excluded from the social fabric of America, there was nothing that legally banned same-sex marriages. Since federal law dictates that a marriage performed in one state is to be recognized in another state, the ruling by the Massachusetts Court had national implications.

The constitutional question before the Massachusetts Supreme Court challenged the state for using *"its formidable regulatory authority to ban same-sex couples from civil marriages?"* The court ruled the state did not have legal grounds upon which to do that.

Chief Justice Margaret H. Marshall separated the secular role of the state from the religious battles that have made gay marriage the new hotly debated social issue for citizens and politicians in America. Chief Justice Marshall wrote:

> *"Many people hold deep-seated religious, moral, and ethical convictions and that homosexual conduct is immoral. Many hold equally strong religious, moral and ethical convictions that same-sex couples are entitled to be married, and that homosexual persons should be treated no differently than their heterosexual neighbors. Neither view answers the question before us."*

Chief Justice Marshall based the decision on the law and not emotion, when she wrote, *"The court was asked to decide on the civil, not religious, aspect of marriage."* A majority of the justices ruled there was no constitutional justification for denying same-sex couples *"the protections, benefits, and obligations of civil marriages"* if denial is based only on their sexual orientation. Justice John M. Greaney wrote in his opinion:

> *"as a matter of constitutional law, neither the mantra of tradition, nor individual conviction, can justify the perpetuation of a hierarchy in which couples of the same sex and their families are deemed less worthy of social and legal recognition than couples of the opposite sex and their families."*

The year 2004 was only six days old when the battle against gay marriage began to gain momentum. On January 6, 2004, conservative groups protested Massachusetts's lawmakers in a statehouse meeting room. The protest was organized to denounce the state Supreme Court's ruling that a ban on gay marriage in the state was unconstitutional. About 200 conservatives demanded the state pass a constitutional amendment that would *ban* gay marriage.

Bishop Gilbert Thompson, a Boston pastor and member of the Black Ministerial Alliance, said, *"The radical sexual revolution will destroy a road map that our children desperately need."* Why is it that so many people who oppose gay marriage make ridiculous predictions about our society smoldering in the wake of the destruction that would certainly be caused by gay marriage? Do not accept Bishop Thompson's prediction that a "radical sexual revolution" will destroy "a road map that our children desperately need." His prediction is nothing more than religious fear mongering.

Too many people openly accept statements from religious leaders as if those statements came directly from God. There is no evidence that the road map left to our children will be destroyed or that our children will be led down the wrong path if gay marriage were to become reality.

In early 2004, the state of Ohio took steps to fend off gay marriage in the future. On January 21, 2004, Ohio lawmakers gave final approval to a bill that would not only ban gay marriage, but would also prohibit state employees from receiving benefits for domestic partners. To date, that was the most restrictive bill of its kind because it went so far as to ban benefits for domestic partners.

After the House approved the bill, the vote in the Senate did not make any kind of overwhelming statement against gay marriage. The Senate vote was 18-15. Ohio Governor Bob Taft anxiously signed the bill into law.

The measure stated that same-sex marriage was against the strong public policy of the state. It also defied a 1934 U.S. Supreme Court ruling that requires states to recognize marriages from other states. The state of Ohio may find itself defending the newly passed bill in front of the U.S. Supreme Court. Strong public policy does not always make for just laws.

The bill passed by the Ohio legislature had been under consideration since 1997. Approval of the measure at the beginning of 2004 was another indication of a growing backlash against the homosexual community, following recent court rulings that brought the possibility of legal gay marriage closer to reality. Ohio State Senator Eric Fingerhut, a Democrat, said the bill would impede

Ohio's progress by essentially putting up a sign that reads, *"We don't want you here."* On Election Day 2004, the citizens of Ohio passed the strict anti-gay bill.

Did the Ohio legislature not understand that the U.S. Supreme Court's ruling that Colorado's Amendment 2 was unconstitutional established a legal precedent that a majority public opinion within a state *does not* protect laws that are unconstitutional? Citizens of Ohio, along with many other states, should be preparing to spend tax dollars on legal challenges to any new state laws that discriminate against the personal beliefs of a majority.

"Will you marry me? I want the benefits!"

I wasn't surprised by the opinions of gay males drinking and watching NFL football on a big-screen TV in a gay bar, but I was surprised by the immediate and definitive answers they gave to the question: Should gays and lesbians have the right to legal marriage? *"Anything less is unacceptable,"* was the instant reaction from Chip, a distinguished-looking gentleman wearing very fashionable clothes and designer glasses. He continued, *"There is no logical argument against it."*

Andrew, a thirty-something senior executive, was quite flamboyant and loquacious. While sipping a cocktail at the bar, Andrew said that gays should *"absolutely"* have the right to legal marriage. But Andrew went on to explain *why* gays want the right to get married in the first place. Andrew said that a gay man would want to marry his gay male partner for the same reason a straight guy would marry his girlfriend: *"It's more emotional than legal. It's more about love."*

A majority of heterosexuals in America believe that granting homosexuals the right to form a "civil union" should be satisfactory to homosexuals. So why the big push for the right to marriage? In addition to equal benefits associated with marriage, gay men and lesbians also want to manifest their love by making a commitment through the institutionalized tradition of marriage. *"Someone gets married because they love another person,"* Andrew explained. He said no one, straight or gay, says, *"I want a tax benefit!"* It shouldn't be so difficult for all heterosexuals to understand that gay marriage is about love, not simply the desire to share legal benefits. When I asked Chip if he thought same-sex marriage would become legal in America, he said, *"It depends on the election in '04."* I'm sure Chip has lost confidence that gay marriage will be legalized any time soon. But Chip and others need to know that opinions towards gay marriage will change before Bush leaves the White House in 2009.

Conservatives *love* the gay marriage debate

President George W. Bush raised the issue of gay marriage in his State of the Union address on January 21, 2004. Below is the text from the President's address that dealt with gay marriage:

> *"A strong America must also value the institution of marriage. I believe we should respect individuals as we take a principled stand for one of the most fundamental, enduring institutions of our civilization. Congress has already taken a stand on this issue by passing the Defense of Marriage Act, signed in 1996 by President Clinton. That statute protects marriage under federal law as a union of a man and a woman, and declares that one state may not redefine marriage for other states. Activist judges, however, have begun redefining marriage by court order, without regard for the will of the people and their elected representatives. On an issue of such great consequence, the people's voice must be heard. If judges insist on forcing their arbitrary will upon the people, the only alternative left to the people would be the constitutional process. Our nation must defend the sanctity of marriage. The outcome of this debate is important—and so is the way we conduct it. The same moral tradition that defines marriage also teaches that each individual has dignity and value in God's sight."*

In any election year, the State of the Union address is more of a campaign speech than an assessment of the state of our nation. The words used to establish President Bush's campaign position on gay marriage were well crafted. The president opposed gay marriage, while saying that homosexuals have *"dignity and value in God's sight."* The Religious Right believes that homosexuals and their innate behavior are condemned in the *eyes of God*.

By using the phrase *"in God's sight,"* President Bush satisfied conservatives by saying that homosexuals had *"dignity and value in God's sight."* This was a subtle but important distinction from the more specific words *in the eyes of God*.

The argument that Christians should love and accept homosexuals but condemn homosexual behavior is a way for Christians to feel Christian-like while implying that homosexuality is a pathway to hell. An individual denying his/her intrinsic sexual tendencies by never participating in homosexual behavior is *not* a homosexual. To say that one can accept the homosexual but not the homosexual behavior is akin to saying that one likes football players who don't play football!

President Bush originally appeared to oppose a constitutional amendment banning gay marriage, but in March of 2004, Bush defined his position by declaring his support of an amendment that would ban same-sex marriage in America. Bush stated that if activist judges fail to respect the will of the American people, then the only answer may lie in the *"constitutional process."*

Truth be known, Republicans are more reluctant than Democrats to support changing the Constitution. President Bush's speechwriters were also brilliant to remind the American people that the issue of protecting the current definition of marriage was actually supported by President Clinton, who signed the Defense of Marriage Act in 1996.

There was another part of Bush's comments on gay marriage in his State of the Union Address of 2004 that deserves a closer look. The President criticized *"activist judges"* for redefining marriage against the will of the American people and their elected officials. My recollection of civics reminds me that it is the Judicial Branch of government that interprets the Constitution and the laws passed by the Legislative Branch. Since the Legislative Branch is made up of representatives voted for by the people, then it is that branch of government that acts on behalf of the people of America. That makes politics the driving motivation behind legislation.

The function of the Judicial Branch of government is to interpret laws and the Constitution without consideration for politics or public opinion polls. Bush's use of the phrase *"the will of the people"* reflects the public opinion polls, which show that a majority of Americans oppose gay marriage. Bush suggested in his address that America take a vote of the people whenever a court ruling disagrees with mass public opinion. And when Bush criticized "activist judges," he was also criticizing a U.S. Supreme Court made up of seven out of nine justices appointed by Republican presidents!

The civil rights battle over gay rights, especially gay marriage, has become the new social issue for conservatives. Taking a definite stance on gay rights, now and in the future, will help define political candidates; not only for the homosexual community, but also for the straight Americans who support gay rights.

Politicians should look beyond the actual numbers of the groups they are appealing to and consider how voters outside of a group feel about attitudes towards the way a group is treated. For example, African Americans account for approximately 13 percent of the U.S. population; however, many millions of white Americans would not support any politician who would support discrimination of African Americans. The same will be true with the issue of gay rights. The homosexual population is realistically believed to be somewhere between 2 percent and 5 percent of the overall population. That is a small voting group set in the context of the entire U.S. population. But many millions of heterosexual voters would not tolerate discrimination against the homosexual minority.

The majority of Americans may not yet support the idea of gay marriage, but a majority of Americans do support tolerance towards the gay community. Because of the great compassion of most Americans politicians must also consider that the realistic size of any minority group also consists of individuals outside of the group. Those voters are equally as important as the actual members of any minority group.

Following the Massachusetts Supreme Court ruling on gay marriage, President Bush issued a statement that read, in part, *"Marriage is a sacred institution between a man and a woman. I will work with congressional leaders and others to do what is legally necessary to defend the sanctity of marriage."* Again, the President addressed the issue of a constitutional amendment banning gay marriage. President Bush wants to satisfy his conservative base, which is not always easy under the umbrella of Bush's "compassionate conservative" image.

Politicians often sacrifice their own political integrity for the sake of appealing to voters. The job of a politician is to get elected or re-elected, rather than do what is right. Polls taken after the Massachusetts Supreme Court ruling showed somewhere between 55 and 60 percent of Americans were opposed to gay marriages. That reaction was an immediate backlash to the ruling that a state's constitution did not actually prohibit gay marriage. And that was only the beginning of the backlash.

Several months before the first presidential primary, the Democratic presidential candidates reacted to the Massachusetts ruling. It would seem logical for the Democratic candidates to support the liberal concept of gay marriage, but the majority opinion from the Democratic field reflected just how much America had moved toward the middle. For a Democratic presidential nominee to win a presidential election, now and in the foreseeable future, he or she must win support of liberal and conservative moderates, as well as independents. To win over the conservative southern Democrats, who think more like Republicans, the Democratic nominee must be divorced from any extreme liberal ideology. Former Georgia Governor Jimmy Carter won enough of the moderate vote in 1976 primarily because of his southern appeal. In 1992 and 1996, Bill Clinton won because he appealed to moderate voters and the South. In 2000, George W. Bush arguably beat Al Gore by winning the moderate and Southern vote. Bush won re-election because of his southern appeal and because Democrat John Kerry was so liberal.

Liberalism died in 1988 with Democratic presidential candidate Michael Dukakis. Clinton defied the liberal left and ran as a "moderate" Democrat in 1992. True conservatism died at the close of the Reagan years in 1988. Today, Democrats and Republicans commit political suicide by aligning themselves with the liberal left or the conservative right. For this reason, those who support gay marriage will not find many high-ranking political allies.

Ronald Reagan was a political phenomenon unto himself. A former actor with incredible charisma who was governor of the state that has the most electoral votes seemed destined to reflect a changing America. There was a general loss of confidence in America's global status after Iran took American citizens working in Iran hostage. That was Iran's way of showing a lack of respect for America's military might.

Under President Jimmy Carter the United States was unable to negotiate the release of the hostages or succeed in a rescue mission. President Carter's ability to be a strong leader in foreign affairs caused the country to turn to the reassuring father-like appeal of Ronald Reagan. George Bush (Sr.) rode the coattails of Reagan and the conservative movement that continued long enough for him to win the election in 1988, but not long enough for him to win re-election in 1992.

In response to the Massachusetts Supreme Court ruling that prohibiting same-sex couples was unconstitutional, Missouri Congressman Dick Gephardt, one of the leading presidential candidates at the time, said that he supported gay unions but opposed gay marriage.

Gephardt said he supported a state's right to decide whether gay marriage should be legal. That sounds like a politician trying to play both sides. In a statement, Gephardt said, *"As we move forward, it is my hope that we don't get sidetracked by the right wing into a debate over a phony constitutional amendment banning gay marriages."* Doesn't that sound like Dick Gephardt *supported* gay marriage? The candidate said he was *against* gay marriage, but warned that Republicans may force a debate over a phony constitutional amendment banning gay marriages. How do these guys sleep at night?

Democratic candidate retired General Wesley Clark, an early contender in 2004, said that as president, he would *"support giving gays and lesbians the legal rights that married couples get, but each state must decide, not the courts."* So, Wesley Clark supported gay couples having all the rights heterosexual couples have, but he also supported the states having the right to pass legislation *prohibiting* gay marriages. The voting public needs to better understand this game politicians play. They play the game because it works. Don't blame the politicians for playing the game; blame us for allowing them to play it!

Senator Joe Lieberman, a conservative Democrat, said of the Massachusetts ruling on gay marriage, *"Although I am opposed to gay marriage, I have also long believed that states have the right to adopt for themselves laws that allow same sex unions. I will oppose any attempt by the right wing to change the Constitution in response to the (Massachusetts ruling), which would be unnecessary and divisive."* So, Lieberman opposed gay marriages but also opposed any attempts by Republicans to change the Constitution to prohibit gay marriages. Here's what that means: Lieberman was trying to attract Democrat and Republican voters. The sad truth is that the majority of the American voters will not pick up on these types of contradictions, which is much more disturbing than the legalization of gay marriage.

Democratic presidential candidate **Senator John Kerry** responded to legal gay marriages saying, *"While I continue to oppose gay marriage, I believe that (the Massachusetts) decision calls on the Massachusetts state legislature to take action to ensure equal protection for gay couples. These protections are long overdue."* What Kerry was actually saying was, "I don't really oppose gay marriage, but I'm trying to appeal to all voters by not really taking a firm stance."

Then-Democratic presidential candidate and former Vermont **Governor Howard Dean** responded to the Massachusetts ruling by saying that, as president, he would sign the nation's first law establishing civil unions for same-sex couples. Dean, by far the most liberal of the potential candidates in 2004, said that he supported civil unions, but not gay marriage.

Just before the Iowa caucuses, Howard Dean said in Iowa that as governor of Vermont he signed the civil union law because of his Christian faith. While on the campaign trail in Iowa, Dean said, *"If God had thought homosexuality is a sin, he would not have created gay people."* The Reverend Martyn Minns of the American Anglican Council responded with, *"It's a very shallow understanding of creation"* to believe that the presence of homosexuals justifies the behavior.

The Reverend Minns said that Dean *"seems confused about a number of things."* Minns went on to say, *"There's a lot of brokenness in this world, and part of the gospel is to come into a place of brokenness and bring healing and transformation."* The comments from the Reverend Minns were a typical response to the acceptance of homosexuality as a normal part of life. I think Dean was right when he implied that God created homosexuals as part of His world.

Senator John Edwards, who would become John Kerry's V-P running mate, said he opposed gay marriage. At least Senator Edwards let us know where he really stood on the issue. Other early presidential candidates in 2004, **Senator Dennis Kucinich** and the **Reverend Al Sharpton** said they supported gay marriage. Kucinich and Sharpton should be congratulated for their decisive stance on a controversial issue most politicians tried to avoid. However, Kucinich and Sharpton faced such slim odds at winning the nomination that each could afford to be honest. If either candidate had a real chance of winning, their opinions would have been tailored to reflect the opinion of the majority of Americans. That's sad, but true.

Former Illinois **Senator Carol Moseley-Braun,** another presidential candidate in 2004, said that discrimination against same-sex couples is wrong, but she did not specifically mention gay marriage. That is a politician who thinks discrimination against gays is wrong, but doesn't want to say that gay marriage should be legal. That takes courage, doesn't it?

The politics of gay marriage

The only actual difference between heterosexuals and homosexuals is the style of sex enjoyed in privacy. In every other way, heterosexuals and homosexuals are identical. If the U.S. Supreme Court has already ruled that gay sex is legal, then shouldn't gay Americans be accepted as normal, functioning members of society?

Further proving that even the Democrats won't always stand up for a minority group when public opinion opposes doing so, President Clinton in 1996 signed the Defense of Marriage Act, which denied federal recognition of gay marriage and gave states the power to ignore same-sex unions licensed in other states. There should be little doubt that Bill Clinton, a true liberal at heart but a political moderate, personally supported gay marriage. Clinton's support of the Defense of Marriage Act was inspired by politics and not personal beliefs.

Anticipating the coming war over gay marriage, a proposed constitutional amendment defining marriage as a "union of a man and a woman" was introduced in the Senate on November 27, 2003. Senator Wayne Allard (R-Colorado) was the sponsor of the amendment. But he was not alone. Republicans Sam Brownback of Kansas and Jeff Sessions of Alabama were co-sponsors. The proposed constitutional amendment would give state legislatures the power to grant benefits to same-sex couples, but would prohibit courts from requiring the granting of benefits. The proposed amendment was introduced in the House, where it had 100 co-sponsors.

The action in the U.S. Senate followed the Massachusetts Supreme Court's ruling that a ban on same-sex marriage was unconstitutional. The speed with which many politicians were getting in line to be part of the effort to legally ban same-sex marriage emphasizes the tough road ahead in the battle for gay marriage. Remember that the fourth year of each decade is the year in which trends that will define the decade begin to come into focus. The major battle lines in the war over gay marriage were drawn in 2004.

A congressional vote on the Federal Marriage Amendment took place in 2004, but the issue of gay marriage had already become part of the presidential campaign before the close of 2003.

"Gay marriage could dominate 2004 elections" was a front-page headline in *The Denver Post* on Sunday, December 21, 2003. Conservative groups were already planning to sponsor efforts to "get out the vote" to support a constitutional ban on gay marriage. Conservative groups went so far as to suggest that the gay marriage issue could become the single issue they focus on in 2004. As the conservatives announced battle plans, gay rights groups were going public with their plans.

Gay rights organizations promised to keep a "score card" on all of the 2004 presidential candidates so voters would know which candidates opposed gay marriage. At the 2004 Gay Pride Festivals across the country there were massive voter registration drive. Those participating in Gay Pride Week were seen as voters likely, okay certain, to vote against Bush! *"You have the potential for an issue that can take over a campaign,"* was a quote from Matthew Spalding from the conservative Heritage Foundation.

The gay marriage issue was a much talked about campaign issue in 2004, but it did not rise to the level of becoming a defining issue. The war in Iraq and the war on terrorism became the top campaign issues. The economy and health care were next.

With the war in Iraq and the war on terrorism dominating the 2004 campaign rhetoric, one has to wonder why so many conservatives believed the gay marriage issue would become "an issue that can take over a campaign."

Even at the height of the controversy in the summer of 2003 and early 2004, the gay marriage issue never had the potential to become a top campaign issue. But conservative Christian Republicans were hoping that the gay marriage issue would become a major campaign issue so it could be used to accentuate the Republicans as the moral party and that President Bush was the better choice for standing up for morality in America. The interest in gay marriage becoming one of the top issues in 2004 was driven by the partisan goal of conservative Republicans advancing their right-wing agenda.

The **Concerned Women for America** organization announced it would launch a campaign on the importance of marriage and why it should be protected. The group was to use newspaper ads, bumper stickers, and articles on its Web site to promote its support of a constitutional amendment defining marriage as a union between a man and a woman only. Considering the current divorce rate among heterosexuals, the **Concerned Women for America** should launch a campaign promoting the importance of marriage and why *heterosexual* couples should protect it.

If a group like **Concerned Women for America** were actually interested in protecting marriage in America, then instead of condemning gay marriage wouldn't a campaign to educate heterosexuals about the importance of marriage yield a far greater impact on the institution of marriage and American society? The actual number of homosexuals who would legally marry is minute compared to the greater number of heterosexuals who get married and then divorced. Heterosexuals have turned marriage into a disposable institution.

If the real intent were to "protect marriage," **Concerned Women for America**, as well as conservative and religious organizations, would better advance their agenda by focusing on heterosexual marriage rather than fight homosexual marriage. But protecting marriage in America is not their agenda. The real agenda of groups like **Concerned Women for America** is promoting the condemnation of homosexuals.

In the debate over gun control, a strict interpretation of the Constitution is deployed to argue in favor of the right citizens have to own a gun. If the Second Amendment were translated literally in the context of the times in which it was conceived, the right to own a gun in America could be easily challenged. The group that would argue *in favor* of strict interpretation of the Constitution to guarantee the right to own a gun is the same group that would argue *against* strict interpretation of the Constitution if it were to lead to legalizing gay marriage. This is also the group that promotes literal interpretation of Biblical scripture in condemning homosexuality, yet ignores scripture that lends credibility to the support of homosexuality. The Constitution and the Bible cannot be used in that manner if either is to be respected.

It is the deep concern that *strict* interpretation of the U.S. Constitution will lead to a U.S. Supreme Court ruling that the Constitution does not contain specific language prohibiting gay marriage that fuels the determination to pass an amendment defining marriage as a union between a man and a woman only. The ruling by the state Supreme Court in Massachusetts, which declared that gay marriage was not unconstitutional, combined with the U.S. Supreme Court ruling that gay sex was constitutional, have caused many conservatives to conclude the next step will be a ruling that *any* ban on same-sex marriage is unconstitutional.

How important was the issue of gay marriage in the 2004 Presidential Election? Glenn Stanton of the conservative Christian group, **Focus on the Family**, believed the fight against legal gay marriage would be one of the big issues that would define the election of 2004. Stanton confirmed the fear that gay marriage could become a reality by saying, *"The very serious concern could not be overstated."*

As 2003 came to a close, national polls showed that a majority of Americans opposed gay marriage. Expect that trend to begin changing in the very near future. In the past, local and national conservative politicians won the support of the anti-abortion conservative right by openly proclaiming a pro-life position on the abortion issue. Candidates failing to make a political promise to fight against legal abortion in America were not given full support of the conservative right. After the general population became fed up with a small, but fanatical, faction of the population attempting to inflict their religious beliefs on others, the abortion issue died as a campaign issue for Republicans running for national office.

After the election of 1992, it became obvious that a woman's right to choose was considered a personal decision, rather than a decision to be made by politicians. Today, the abortion issue is no longer a litmus test for politicians, much to the disappointment of the conservative right.

How will Bush's re-election impact gay marriage?

The re-election of Bush will cause many people to switch from opposing gay marriage to supporting it. The Bush victory will be seen by conservatives as a mandate to push for a stronger conservative agenda. This will accentuate the attempt by conservatives to change America into a nation dominated by the beliefs of the Christian Right. When that begins to develop—and it most certainly will—many will take another look at the gay marriage issue. Supporting gay marriage will become a way for many Americans to express their opposition to the promotion of a conservative right agenda.

The reality that gay marriage could become an accepted part of our cultural tradition began to get attention in 2000 when the state of Vermont passed a "civil union law," which granted the rights of traditional marriages to same-sex couples, but not the right to legal marriage. The idea of extending **rights** granted to individuals married to same-sex partners was not a threat to our cultural norms. Those opposing homosexuality were concerned about gay couples receiving the rights and benefits male/female heterosexual couples received; but they were satisfied that gay couples were not given the right to legal marriage.

The concept of civil unions may have once seemed like the ultimate dream of same-sex couples, but once that goal was attained, the demand for equal rights, including marriage, further motivated the gay community's crusade for greater equality.

It is no coincidence that the battle over same-sex marriage became an issue towards the end of a Republican president's first term. Forcing the issue of gay marriage into the political arena was the gay community's backlash against a growing conservative trend inspired by a Republican White House. Rights or opportunities not shared by the more liberal segment of society will always be accentuated when considered within the context of a White House occupied by a Republican. Conversely, the prominence of conservative issues grows during the term of a Democratic president. We are once again an extremely divided nation with no sight of unity on the horizon.

With a divorce rate believed to be near 50 percent, heterosexuals are in no position to pass judgment on whether or not homosexuals should have the right to marry. If one out of every two marriages ends in divorce, then heterosexuals don't have much credibility when it comes to the legal commitment of marriage. There is some dispute over the figure of 50 percent of all marriages ending in divorce. Some experts believe the actual divorce rate may be closer to 21 percent. Even at the lower percentage, heterosexuals have nothing to be proud of when it comes to the institution of marriage and the permanent impact divorce has had on America.

Before the end of 2003, President Bush's opposition to gay marriage became more definitive. On December 16, 2003, Bush announced in Washington that *"we may need a constitutional amendment"* defining marriage as a union between a man and a woman. Prior to that, Bush had not been specific on the idea of a new constitutional amendment. The president did condemn the ruling by the Massachusetts Supreme Court in November 2003, but did not go so far as to announce his support for changing the Constitution. Bush described the state court as *"a very activist court in making the decision it made,"* and said the court went beyond its bounds and *"did the job of the Legislature."*

Maybe President Bush needs a refresher course in basic civics. It *is* the job of a state Supreme Court, as part of the Judicial Branch of government, to interpret a state's constitution and the laws passed by the Legislative Branch of government. Our Constitution has a history of providing more freedom to individuals, rather than taking it away.

The year 2004 was still young when the *Denver Post* ran this headline on the front page of the edition on Sunday, January 11, 2003: **"VP would back ban on gay marriage."**

In an interview with the *Denver Post,* Vice President Dick Cheney talked about the continuing war in Iraq and U.S. soldiers continuing to be killed and injured, energy issues in the Western states, the sex scandal at the Air Force Academy, and his support of an amendment banning gay marriage.

Of all the things the vice president discussed in that interview, the newspaper considered the headline about Cheney's support of an amendment prohibiting gay marriage to be the most compelling. Every other issue the vice president addressed in the interview had a far greater impact on America than the gay marriage issue. But sex sells everything, including newspapers. Since sexual activity is the only difference between homosexuals and heterosexuals, sex will always be part of any debate involving homosexuality.

During the presidential campaign of 2000, candidate Cheney was asked about gay marriage. Cheney responded by talking about America's free society and that *"freedom means freedom for everyone."* He went on to say that individuals should be *"free to enter into any kind of relationship"* and that others should not attempt to regulate or prohibit anyone's relationship decisions. America was a different nation during the presidential campaign of 2000 and expressing support of the freedoms extended to homosexuals was not politically damaging.

But Vice President Cheney changed his opinion on the government getting involved in the personal and sexual relationships of individuals. Cheney also changed his stance on how relationships should be regulated.

While responding to the question of gay marriage during the 2000 campaign, Cheney said that the legal status of gay marriage should be left up to each state, not the federal government. But at the beginning of 2004, when the gay marriage issue was becoming a major campaign issue, the vice president said he *would* support a federal ban on gay marriage if President Bush took that stance, which he did just a few weeks later.

35

Then Cheney changed his mind again! About two months before Election Day 2004 Cheney parted with President Bush and said that he no longer supported a constitutional amendment defining marriage as a union between a man and woman only. During the 2004 campaign, Bush and the Republicans constantly labeled John Kerry a "flip-flopper," saying that his opinions and voting record in the Senate were constantly changing. Why Kerry and the Democrats did not turn the tables and label Cheney a "flip-flopper" remains a mystery to me. Unless Kerry was *suppose* to lose in 2004 so Hillary could run in 2008!

The abortion issue was a key political issue, but a majority of Americans reached a point where they were fed up with pro-life groups pushing for government intervention regarding a very personal decision. For Republican candidates, opposing a woman's right to choose had become an act of political suicide. The gay marriage issue will follow the same pattern. The fight to allow the government to get involved in the personal decision of marriage, even between two homosexuals, will reach a point where a majority of Americans will conclude that gay marriage is a decision to be made by two consenting individuals, not the government.

On December 21, 2003, the *New York Times* released a poll showing that a majority of Americans supported a constitutional amendment banning gay marriage. The poll showed 55 percent of those surveyed favored an amendment that would define marriage as a union between a man and a woman, while 40 percent opposed the idea of the amendment.

`Here is what else the poll showed about America's opinions on aspects of gay rights.

Should homosexual relationships between adults be:
Legal: 41%
Not Legal: 49%
No Opinion: 9%

Men: (Legal) 40%
Women: (Legal) 49%
No Opinion: 8%

18-24 years old:
Legal: 58%
Not Legal: 39%
No Opinion: 3%

30-44 years old:
Legal: 43%
Not Legal: 48%
No Opinion: 9%

45-64 years old:
Legal: 38%
Not legal: 52%
No Opinion: 10%

65 and older:
Legal: 24%
Not Legal: 61%
No Opinion: 15%

Do you favor or oppose a law allowing homosexuals to marry?
Favor: 34%
Oppose: 61%
No Opinion: 5%

Men: (Favor) 30%
Men: (Oppose) 65%

Women: (Favor) 38%
Women: (Oppose) 57%

Do you favor or oppose a constitutional amendment defining marriage as a union between a man and a woman only?
Favor: 55%
Oppose: 40%
Men: (Favor) 57%
Men: (Oppose) 39%

Women: (Favor) 54%
Women: (Oppose) 42%

Since the poll was taken *after* the Massachusetts Supreme Court ruling, which presumably opened the door to legal gay marriage, it reflected what seemed to be a new backlash against the gay community. The poll showed America's reaction to the real possibility that a cultural tradition might be eliminated.

One of the primary reasons many Americans oppose gay marriage has nothing to do with discrimination against homosexuals. The rapidly changing world around us manifests feelings of insecurity, as many established traditions are lost to new norms. The pace of the changes caused by new technology and computers leaves humans with an instinct to cling to traditions that create a sense of stability. Subconsciously, many people oppose gay marriage out of fear of losing a tradition, not the fear of what adverse effect gay marriage will have on society.

Prior to the Massachusetts State Supreme Court ruling that the state's constitution did not include wording specifically prohibiting same-sex marriage, it was easier for a majority of Americans to support gay marriage because it didn't seem likely to become a reality. Change in deep traditions manifests insecurity, which leads to an instinct to resist change.

As the poll shows, more men than women oppose homosexual adults having sex. Let me state the obvious: Straight men, as a group, would welcome the opportunity to watch two women having sex with each other, but would be repulsed by the idea of two men having sex. So are straight men for or against homosexual activity?

Compare the reaction men have to gay sex to the many straight women who are not only more open to the idea of sex with another women but may also be interested in watching two men have sex. This may seem hypocritical, but it reveals the innate sexual differences between males and females.

Many heterosexual men enjoy watching two women having sex because of a subconscious desire to learn what precisely satisfies women. Women are more sexually intricate. Also, watching two women together allows straight men to *watch* others having sex without the involvement of a male penis. That's an important issue for the great majority of heterosexual men.

Unlike heterosexual men, heterosexual women are more prone to admit they might enjoy watching what two men do to sexually satisfy each other. There is something sexually educational about observing two members of the same gender engaging in sex. And many heterosexual women are openly curious about experiencing sex with another woman. A great number of typical women in America have a subconscious, if not a conscious, sense that only another woman would really know how to satisfy them sexually. Ask straight women how often they have been with straight men that had no idea what to do!

The aforementioned poll shows that more men than women oppose a law legalizing same-sex marriage and support a constitutional amendment defining marriage as a union between a man and a woman. Opposition to homosexual sex, same-sex marriage, and an amendment banning same-sex marriage grows as the age of those responding increases. Younger minds are more willing to accept change because traditions and habits have not become as deep-rooted in their lives. The promotion and acceptance of political and social issues are governed by the same marketing principles that control the marketing of any product.

The marketing of gay rights

While trying to reach younger beer drinkers, beer companies have been accused of targeting underage drinkers. Advertising that targets younger beer drinkers, 21-25 for example, will obviously be designed to attract the attention of younger beer drinkers, but that does not necessarily mean the beer companies are actually targeting underage drinkers. Most seventeen and eighteen-year-olds want to be older, which leads them to instinctively respond to beer advertising that targets beer drinkers over twenty-one. Any type of advertising can miss a demographic target, but that does not determine intent. Beer companies are unfairly criticized for purposely trying to encourage underage drinking.

Look at this from the perspective of the beer companies. Which group do you think would be more willing to try a certain beer, a new twenty-one-year-old beer drinker or a fifty-five-year-old beer drinker? Chances are the fifty-five-year-old beer drinker has already established what is known as "brand loyalty." That means over the years, the habit of buying a certain brand of beer has become such a tradition that the chances of changing that older consumer's buying habits are much less likely than trying to convince a new, younger beer drinker to sample a certain brand. This is true with most every product or service that is advertised and marketed to consumers.

Opinions about social and political issues are processed in the mind like preferences for consumed products. A younger mind is much more likely to be flexible towards accepting new social and political ideas than a mind that has already been conditioned to judge ideas through habit or tradition. In the poll on same-sex relationships, same-sex marriage, and a constitutional amendment banning same-sex marriage, a majority of the youngest respondents *did not* oppose same-sex marriage and sexual relations and opposed a constitutional amendment banning same-sex marriage.

Women were slightly more willing to accept same-sex relations and same-sex marriage than men were; and more women than men opposed an amendment defining marriage as a union between a man and a woman only. The greatest support for gay rights came from people living in the West, compared to the Northeast, the North Central, and the South. More Democrats and Independents were supportive of gay relations and gay marriage than Republicans; and more Democrats and Independents were opposed to an amendment that would ban same-sex marriage. It is worth noting that Republicans are historically more protective of the Constitution and less willing to support any permanent changes in the form of new amendments. Except in the case of gay marriage, of course.

Here is the political breakout of the poll on gay rights and gay marriage:

Homosexual relations between adults should be....

Legal: Republicans: 34%
Democrats: 46%
Independents: 44%

Not Legal: Republicans: 57%
Democrats: 46%
Independents: 46%

Do you favor or oppose a law allowing homosexuals to marry?

Favor: Republicans: 26%
Democrats: 39%
Independents: 37%

Oppose: Republicans: 71%
Democrats: 57%
Independents: 58%

Do you favor or oppose an amendment defining marriage as a union between a man and a woman only?

Favor: Republicans: 63%
Democrats: 52%
Independents: 51%

Oppose: Republicans: 33%
Democrats: 44%
Independents: 43%

Gay rights organizations were obviously not happy with the results of the *New York Times*/CBS Poll. The results of the poll do conflict with a *USA Today*/CNN/Gallup Poll, which was taken in October of 2003, prior to the Massachusetts Supreme Court ruling on same-sex marriage. In that poll, a majority of respondents from eighteen to sixty years old had no opposition to same-sex marriage.

The methodology of national polls is so scientific the fact that these two polls were sponsored by different organizations is not the reason for the conflicting results. It was the timing of the two polls that produced the differing results. The poll taken before the Massachusetts Supreme Court ruling reflected a greater willingness to accept the idea of same-sex marriage. But when same-sex marriage took a major step towards becoming reality, the collective opinion of America changed.

Teaching students to be gay?

A public school in North Carolina violated the First Amendment when an official of the school encouraged his staff to attend a presentation on homosexuality, which was sponsored by the Christian group, **LIFE** (**L**ife **I**n **F**reedom **E**ternally ministry).

On November 10, 2003, Don Martin, a school official with the Winston-Salem/Forsyth County Schools, was informed that by encouraging his staff to attend a Christian-sponsored presentation on homosexuality, he was, in effect, supporting a specific religious belief on the social issue of homosexuality.

Martin sent an e-mail to his staff promoting the Christian presentation on homosexuality. In the e-mail, Martin mentioned Joanna Highley, founder of the group **LIFE**, who claims to have "worked" with practicing homosexuals on returning to a heterosexual lifestyle. Highley, like many Christian fundamentalists, believes that homosexuality is *"a Satanic counterfeit to God's created design."* It is this myopic religious thinking that requires promoting a greater tolerance of homosexuality in schools. It is comforting to know that even in the state of North Carolina, known more for its tobacco crops than its progressive thinking, a school official was reprimanded for encouraging his staff to attend a presentation on homosexuality.

Promoting further acceptance of homosexuality at the student level is crucial. Same-sex couples are adopting *and* having children. For the children growing up in a same-sex household, as well as the millions of children in America growing up in a single-parent household, our world is different from the way it was when the Baby

Boomer generation was growing up. There is always the temptation for adults to view the world their children see through their own life experiences. What is *real* for a child today was not *real* for a child years ago, but that doesn't mean that children are worse off today. It just means they are different. Gay and lesbian couples raising children is a very controversial aspect of gay rights and gay marriage.

It is important for our schools to adjust to the reality that two parents may not be there for Parent-Teacher Day, or that the two parents may be of the same sex. It is crucial for *all* students to not just tolerate, but to embrace the children who are being raised by same-sex parents. A loving and caring gay parent is better than having no parent at all! Or is it? **(Gay adoption: how does it harm children?** Page 112)

Your mother wears army boots-and she's gay!

Imagine a school so opposed to homosexuality that a student is punished because he told a classmate that his mother was gay. On December 12, 2003, the school board in the southwest Louisiana town of Lafayette announced it would not apologize for punishing Marcus McLaurin for using the word "gay." The school board tried to say that Marcus was punished for behavioral problems and not for using the word "gay." However, a form the school sent home with Marcus explained that he was being punished for using the word "gay." Marcus' mother brought the problem to the ACLU, which demanded an apology from the school.

On December 11, 2003, the school board in Lafayette, Louisiana voted that it was *"never the intent or purpose"* to punish the student for using the word "gay," but offered no other explanation for the punishment. The ACLU described the school board's action as "revisionist history" and considered a lawsuit.

If a school, even in Louisiana Cajun country, is intolerant of a student saying that his mother is "gay," how can the argument be made that actively promoting the tolerance and acceptance of homosexuality in schools is not imperative?

The rights at stake are less historic and the battle is not physical, but the fight over equal rights and acceptance of homosexuals at every level of society does have similarities to the exclusion of blacks from society when the civil rights crusade was gaining strength in the late 1950s and early 1960s. What America learned from the fight for equal rights for blacks was that no one was to be judged because of differences that caused discrimination by a majority. And yet, today's fight over gay rights is about a different lifestyle that has been opposed by a majority of Americans.

Will same-sex marriage destroy society?

Gay marriage will destroy the structure of American society! That is one of the alarming arguments used in the protest of same-sex marriage. In discussing the issue of gay marriage on talk radio, I am quite cognizant of the prevailing opinion that our society would be adversely affected by legal marriages between gays and lesbians. Some argue that such marriages will actually *destroy* society. But I have yet to hear anyone answer the question, *how* will gay marriages destroy or even harm society? The reason no one can answer the question is because gay marriage *will not* destroy our society, regardless of the thousands of years of traditional marriages. The threat of the downfall of society is nothing more than a scare tactic. What's frightening is that many people really do believe gay marriage will destroy society! But they can't tell you how it will happen! Shouldn't that cause everyone to pause?

There is also a fear that gay marriage will lead to a greater number of homosexuals in America. As tolerance for homosexuality has increased, the percentage of the gay and lesbian population has not actually fluctuated. The increasing acceptance of homosexuality in mainstream America has encouraged many gays and lesbians to live their lives more openly, but there are no statistics indicating any noticeable increase in the number of homosexuals. We may never have an accurate count of the percentage of homosexuals in the population thanks to the continuing social stigma attached to homosexuality.

If same-sex marriages will not cause any increase in the size of the homosexual population in America, then what other objections could there be? Legally married homosexual couples would never account for a large enough segment of the overall population to negatively effect society, either morally or economically.

Another argument against same-sex marriage comes in the form of a threat to businesses. Would same-sex marriages and the granting of health and other benefits to these couples hurt America's businesses? Considering that no limit exists on the number of married straight couples that can receive benefits from the government, or the private sector, there is no justification for the argument that granting total benefits to homosexual couples would adversely affect business.

Still another fear expressed by anti-gay activists is the danger of open gay promiscuity! If marriage were an option, married gay couples would have sex in the privacy of their homes-just like straight couples. But that logical reality destroys the rhetoric from those who believe that homosexuals would demonstrate inappropriate behavior in public, therefore setting a bad example for children.

If there were a legitimate reason to believe that gay marriage would have a negative effect on society, those who support gay marriage would surely reconsider their position. I do not believe people would knowingly support any action that could lead to the destruction of our society (terrorists excluded).

After the Texas sodomy law was declared unconstitutional, conservative Justice Antonin Scalia said that gay sex would start a *"massive disruption of the current social order."* But he failed to explain **why** or **how**. Justice Scalia accused fellow Justice Anthony Kennedy, who was appointed to the Court by Ronald Reagan, of having *"largely signed on to the so-called homosexual agenda."* A Supreme Court Justice who was appointed by a conservative Republican president, Ronald Reagan, was accused of signing on to the "homosexual agenda"!

The Reverend Jerry Falwell and Religious Right leader James Dobson, from **Focus on the Family**, agreed that legalizing gay sex was the beginning of legalizing gay marriage. Another Religious Right leader, Pat Robertson and the **Traditional Values Coalition** President Lou Sheldon condemned the high court's ruling. Sheldon made the comment that any Supreme Court Justice who was not a friend of the Religious Right needed to be replaced. Since justices hold their positions for life, was he suggesting that some of the Supreme Court justices be assassinated? The conservative right should have no complaints about the collective decision-making of the Supreme Court, since Republican presidents appointed seven of the nine justices.

Pat Robertson sent a letter to all of his supporters, asking them to join him in crying out to our Lord to *change* the Supreme Court! Was he hoping that God would answer those prayers by causing some of the justices to die?

Robertson was extremely critical of the Court's ruling in *Lawrence v. Texas*. He claimed the Supreme Court ruling established a *"constitutional right to consensual sodomy and, by the language in its decision, has opened the door to homosexual marriage, bigamy, legalized prostitution and incest."* How could granting marriage rights to gays and lesbians lead to "legalized prostitution, bigamy, or incest"? Again no explanation from those making ridiculous predictions.

Prostitution should be legalized under the right to privacy. Two consenting adults should have the legal right to exchange sex for money. Time spent busting prostitutes and johns is a distraction from more important police work.

Unlike gay marriage and prostitution, incest hurts an innocent victim. Preying on a trusting child for personal satisfaction violates the rights of a child too young to give reasonable consent. And if gay marriage were to be legalized, why should that necessarily lead to bigamy?

If gay marriage were legal what would stop a person from marrying two, three, or four wives? That is a popular argument used to protest gay marriage. Maybe the day will come when marriage to multiple spouses will be a necessary issue, but right now we can draw a line at "marriage" being the union between a "couple."

There are lines drawn throughout our society. An American has the right to own a gun, but not every American has the right to carry a gun with them wherever they go. An American has the right to freedom of speech, but there's a line drawn at the use of that freedom to slander another person. Why can't marriage in America be defined as the union of a "couple?" It is not unprecedented to limit certain rights.

Remember, it wasn't too long ago when marriage was defined as the union of a white man and a white woman or a black man and a black woman. As a society we decided to extend the line that was drawn at interracial marriage. There is precedent for allowing gay marriages, but requiring that every marriage be between two adults.

Defending marriage

The Religious Right lacks confidence that the Defense of Marriage Act signed by President Clinton in 1996 would hold up under strict scrutiny by the federal courts. The concern was centered around the possibility that a federal court could strike down the Defense of Marriage Act on grounds that it is in violation of the Fourth Amendment to the Constitution.

The Fourth Amendment requires that *"Full faith and credit shall be given each State to the public Acts, Records, and judicial Proceedings of every other state."* In other words, a legal marriage in one state is to be honored by other states. If one state were to legalize gay marriage then gays and lesbians from all over the country could go to that state, get married, and then return legally married to the state in which they reside. But states are not necessarily required to honor a marriage license from another state.

Challenges will come from those states that have already passed legislation designed to prohibit honoring gay marriages that might be performed in other states. Missouri, the **"show me state,"** became the first state to pass an amendment defining marriage as a union between a man and a woman. It appears the **"show me state"** doesn't want to show everything!

The battle over legal gay marriage has been building for a few years and is now on the verge of becoming a major civil rights battle. In 1999, the Alliance for Marriage began a campaign of *"promoting marriage and addressing the crisis of family disintegration in the U.S."* The tradition of marriage in America is already threatened, but gays and lesbians have *not* had the right to marry legally. Shouldn't the problem of rapidly dissolving marriages be blamed on heterosexuals? There are major problems with the institution of marriage in this country, but how could any of those problems be blamed on a group that has *never* had the legal right to get married?

In 2001, the **Alliance for Marriage** created a Federal Marriage Amendment that would define marriage as a union between a man

47

and a woman. It was introduced in Congress, but in 2001, gay marriage was not a high-profile political or social issue. The Federal Marriage Amendment never received much attention from the lawmakers on Capitol Hill and it remained in committee. However, in the summer of 2003, when the U.S. Supreme Court ruled that prohibiting gay sex was unconstitutional, the issue instantly received new attention from politicians and citizens.

Congresswoman Marilyn Musgrave (R-Colorado) backed the Federal Marriage Amendment. In an interview with **Christianity Today,** Representative Musgrave called on all Christians to fight any attempt to grant homosexuals equality. Does that mean a U.S. Representative in Congress was asking Christians to wage a battle against allowing a minority group of Americans from enjoying total equality? Musgrave said that the fight over gay marriage is a cultural war that Christians cannot lose. Christians are preparing to declare war on gays and all of those who support gay rights.

The **American Family Association** wrote a petition to Congress, which declared that marriage in America should only be between a man and a woman and that is the *"God-ordained building block of the family and bedrock of civil society."* These religious-based groups seem to ignore the reality that *heterosexuals* have turned marriage into a disposable institution.

The **American Family Association** and **Focus on the Family** became partners. (Not in a homosexual way!) James Dobson from **Focus on the Family** asked his entire membership to support any petitions from the **American Family Association.** In an article that appeared in the *Washington Post* on August 17, 2003, there was a report that **Focus on the Family** had plans to spend as much money and energy as necessary in order to defeat any attempt to legalize gay marriage.

Motivated by their religious beliefs, the Christian groups focused so much attention on their crusade against gays and lesbians they ignored those actions that truly have had a negative impact on society. Divorce, unwanted pregnancy, and promiscuity all currently pose a much larger threat to society than gay marriage. The goal of the Christian Right is the condemnation of homosexuals, not realistically assessing what is actually a detriment to American society.

Christian groups could spend money and energy to better teach teenagers about the consequences of casual sex and adults about the consequences of divorce on families. Christian groups could spend time and money teaching teenagers about the harmful effects of drinking or taking drugs. They should spend a lot of time explaining why they are so quick to condemn homosexuals, when one of the most important teachings of Jesus was resisting the judgment of others. Maybe Christians realize they just haven't had a good crusade in recent memory, so why not start one against the homosexual community?

With all the problems in the world, it is shameful that the Christian Right feels so compelled to focus their attention on defeating something that will have absolutely no effect on their lives. *"Children need to grow up in strong male-female headed families, not same-sex communes filled with sexually obsessed drifters,"* was a statement from Lou Sheldon with the **Traditional Values Coalition.** That sounds real nice, but it's far from reality.

How dare these *alleged* Christians make such a blanket statement about the need for children to grow up in a male-female led household? In many situations, divorce is not a decision made by both spouses. Divorce can be the result of the actions and feelings of only one member of the married heterosexual couple.

It is totally unfair for the Religious Right to link their condemnation of homosexual marriage to the importance of male-female led households. Many Christian groups condemn gay marriage because it innately creates non-traditional families. But many Christians who head families as single parents are the head of a non-traditional family.

In July of 2003, during a press conference at the White House, President Bush said he had told the White House lawyers to find a way to "codify" the definition of marriage as a union between a man and a woman. Like President Clinton, who signed the Defense of Marriage Act in 1996, President Bush will always say and do whatever it takes to ensure a political victory. However, make no mistake about the degree to which Bush is motivated by a born-again Christian ideology.

If polls showed that 55-60 percent of the population opposed gay marriage, there is not a politician within our borders who would stand up a take a position contrary to prevailing public opinion. That goes for every issue, not just the issue of gay rights.

In the *Los Angeles Times*, columnist Robert Scheer criticized President Bush for defining marriage as an institution based on religion. Scheer said that the top official of our secular government, President Bush crossed the line when he talked about the sanctity of marriage and sin. *Atlanta Journal-Constitution* journalist Cynthia Tucker wrote that this nation does not need religious conservatives trying to hijack the U.S. Constitution. Maureen Dowd, a syndicated columnist at the *New York Times,* wrote on August 3, 2003, *"Last time I checked, we had separation of church and state, so I don't know why the president is talking about 'sin,' or why he is implying that gays who want to make a permanent commitment in a world full of divorce and loneliness are sinners."*

If gay marriage becomes legal, the door will be further opened to the idea of gay and lesbian couples adopting children. And that leads to another concern about the impact gay marriage might have on America.

Gay adoption: how does it harm children?

A young child is moved from one foster home to another and has no established home and no permanent parents. Is that child better off continuing to be shuffled from one home to another, or being adopted by two caring and loving adults who have made a conscious decision to become parents?

The answer to that question seems obvious. *Any* child's life would be better if the child were in a stable home with permanent loving parents. However, many people would like a little more information about the adopting couple before making that decision. They would be interested in knowing if the two loving and caring parents were homosexual. And should the answer be *"yes,"* then many would argue that a young child would be better off with no permanent home and no permanent set of adult parents, rather than grow up with one or two gay parents. The anti-gay agenda of the Religious Right always supersedes what is in the best interest of a child.

By the end of 2003, a few studies had been released indicating that a majority of adoption agencies supported the idea of homosexual adoption. A Rutgers University study released in March of 2003 found that 63 percent of all public and private adoption agencies supported gay and lesbian adoption. Combine that information with the pro-gay court rulings in 2003 and groups like the **Family Research Council** began to aggressively fight back against the notion that gay adoption should be considered acceptable.

Make no mistake about the agenda of the **Family Research Council,** which has the slogan, "Defending Family, Faith and Freedom." To the Religious Right, one of the greatest threats to America is the mainstream recognition and acceptance of homosexual *families.*

In a press release issued on October 29, 2003, **Family Research Council** President Tony Perkins said, *"Children are not guinea pigs to be used in social experiments that aim to redefine the institutions of marriage and family."* It is important to note that the Rutgers survey on homosexual adoption was funded by The Rainbow Endowment, one of the largest pro-homosexual organizations in America. Perkins called the entire survey *"a fraud."* Part of the evidence he used to discredit the survey was the fact that only 41 percent of the adoption agencies contacted for the study responded. Perkins called that *"a small sample."* Forty-one percent of most polls or studies is actually considered substantial sample.

In the press release attacking the new survey on same-sex adoption, **Family Research Council** President Perkins said that science has already told us that homosexual adoption is scientifically wrong. In the press release, Mr. Perkins made this observation, *"Children raised in homosexual households are more likely to experiment with homosexuality, to be sexually promiscuous, and to have behavioral and many other developmental problems."*

If what Mr. Perkins wrote could be supported with scientific evidence, the majority of adoption agencies in America would not encourage homosexual adoption. If children, who are raised in homosexual households developed problems that children in heterosexual households did not experience, are we sure those problems are the result of homosexual parents? Wouldn't to be logical to assume that children, who are adopted, especially after moving from one foster home to another, might tend to have more behavioral and more developmental problems than the children growing up in stable homes with loving parents might? Far too many people accept the Christian right's theories as fact, when the theories are nothing more than their own form of propaganda.

Perkins' opinion of gay adoption gives the impression that gay adoption activists are more interested in promoting the idea that a homosexual's desire to become a parent is *more* important than what is in the best interest of the child. There is no general trend in the homosexual community to ignore the interest of a child over the desire to become a parent. Quite the opposite is true. The support of homosexual adoption is motivated by the current need for loving parents to adopt children who remain in the system with no permanent home. Homosexuals do not adopt children for the purpose of acquiring a child as a possession.

Homosexual men and women are not given preferential treatment in the adoption process, yet that is the impression one gets from the harsh criticism of the Christian right. No one is arguing that a mother and a father are ideal for raising a child, provided of course, that the heterosexual mother and father are caring and loving parents. But that is simply not part of many children's real world.

FRC President Perkins said in the press release, *"To intentionally deprive [children] of a mother or a father by placing them in homosexual households is unconscionable."* That is the collective attitude of the Christian right. A male father and a female mother raising a child may *appear* to be an appropriate family, but not always. It would seem Mr. Perkins is so concerned about every child being raised by heterosexuals, that little consideration is given to the reality that heterosexual parents abuse their children or neglect their children due to drug and/or alcohol abuse. Being a heterosexual parent does not necessarily make that parent a better father or mother than a homosexual parent. But try to convince that to members of the Christian right.

The **Family Research Council** promotes the idea that giving homosexuals the right to marry and to adopt children is part of a gay agenda that minimizes differences between homosexuals and heterosexuals, so as to make homosexuality appear normal. Other than private sexual actions homosexuals *are* as normal as heterosexuals.

There are currently only three states that have passed statutes specifically prohibiting homosexual adoption. Those states are

Florida, Mississippi, and Utah. The statute in Utah prohibits all unmarried people, even heterosexuals, from adopting. California, Connecticut, Illinois, Massachusetts, New Jersey, New York, Vermont, and the District of Columbia are states that currently permit homosexual adoption. Twenty states allow "second-parent adoptions."

A second-parent adoption is the legal adoption of a child by the same-sex partner of the child's legal parent. Many same-sex couples are currently raising children in their households as the result of a previous heterosexual marriage. This type of adoption is highly criticized by the Christian right.

But there are methods for same-sex couples to have children that are not adopted. Artificial insemination for lesbians, and in the case of gay men, the use of a surrogate mother inseminated with their sperm, both allow homosexuals to become the biological parents of children.

Anti-gay conservative Christians abhor second-parent adoption. The legal fight to prevent gay and lesbian couples from adopting each other's children from previous marriages is expected to escalate. For the second year in a row, the state of Colorado killed a bill that would have allowed same-sex couples to adopt one another's children. *"You might wish we were all Ozzies and Harriets, Junes and Wards. But we have Ozzies and Harrys, Junes and Janes,"* commented State Representative Alice Madden, sponsor of the bill.

A bill that would allow gay and lesbian couples to adopt a partner's child has merit. If a gay partner were allowed to legally adopt a partner's real child, then the child would have a legal parent should something happen to the child's biological parent. The opportunity to adopt a gay partner's child would also provide for the protection of health insurance, Social Security benefits, and inheritance.

"This is all about these little kids," said Doug Henderson who has a same-sex partner. The two men are raising a four-year-old girl and one-year-old twins. Colorado state law requires that every action be in the best interest of the child, but what many conservative Christians believe to be in the best interest of the child changes dramatically when homosexuals provide what really is in the best interest of a child.

Whistleblower magazine put out an edition in July 2003 that dealt with the "secret" gay rights agenda. The contention was that homosexual activists are *targeting* America's children. *"It's time to acknowledge that homosexual behavior threatens the foundation of Western civilization—the nuclear family,"* writes Steve Baldwin. He continues to support his premise with, *"Research confirms that homosexuals molest children at a rate vastly higher than heterosexuals and the mainstream homosexual culture commonly promotes sex with children."* That is totally inaccurate right-wing rhetoric that cannot be supported by *any* legitimate research.

I have *never* heard one of my many gay or lesbian acquaintances speak of a desire to have sex with children; or that as homosexuals they *target* children. And I know of no evidence that homosexuals molest children at a higher rate than heterosexuals. Molestation, like rape, is less about sex and more about power and control.

The *truth* about homosexuals and pedophiles-it may surprise you!

Many heterosexuals have a basic and unshakable concept of what constitutes homosexual sex. For example, if a man has sex with a young male, then the man must be a homosexual. Wrong! This is one of the great misconceptions about pedophiles and homosexuals.

A pedophile is a person whose primary sexual attraction is to children. That's the definition offered by *Wikipedia Encyclopedia.* There is no mention of sexual orientation in the definition.

Linking pedophilia to homosexuality has been used by the Christian right to define homosexuals as sexual perverts and deviants and therefore, they are a danger to our children. Pedophiles and homosexuals are *"certainly two distinct things,"* was a quote from James Hord, a psychologist who appeared in a press release from **The National Organization for Women.** Hord specializes in the treatment of sexually abused children. Hord explains that many heterosexual pedophiles prefer boys to girls, but the attraction has much more to do with age than gender.

Mental health professionals do not consider a man who is sexually attracted to male children to be a homosexual. He is a *pedophile*. This is difficult for many heterosexuals to comprehend, since a male's attraction to another male is understood to be the most basic definition of homosexuality.

The words "sexually attracted," as used to describe pedophiles, do not mean the sexual attraction is similar to the sexual attraction of teenagers with other teenagers or adults with adults. Joe Zychik overcame pedophilia. Joe says that as a pedophile, he was actually looking for opportunities to *control* children and not opportunities to *satisfy* a sexual urge. By targeting children to fulfill a desire to control another person, a pedophile reduces the chances of rejection.

Pedophiles are adults who may be having a difficult time dealing with people their own age. Insecurity and stress in an adult relationship can also cause an adult to be sexually attracted to children. Seeking power and control in a relationship, the pedophile finds that children are a way of satisfying those desires. Insecurity is another fundamental element of pedophilia. Since the manifestation of the pedophile's desire to control is physical sex, the physical nature of the sex act disguises the real psychological reasons.

Pedophiles can be divided into three categories. After eighteen years of assessing and treating sex offenders, Dr. Howard Barbaree of the Clarke Institute of Psychiatry in Toronto, Canada concludes there are **true pedophiles, opportunistic child molesters,** and **incest offenders**. The last two are not true pedophiles; they take advantage of an opportunity presented to them. Dr. Barbaree's research found *no* evidence that homosexuals are more likely to molest children than heterosexuals.

Is the Christian *right* about pedophilia and homosexuality?

A study at the University of Colorado in Boulder discovered that a child is 100 times more likely to be molested by a heterosexual than a homosexual! A U.S. study of 209 child abuse cases yielded only 2 that involved gay or bisexual offenders.

The perpetrators of child sexual abuse are overwhelmingly heterosexual males, but a few are women. The molester of a child is most often a member of the child's family or someone who is known to the family. Molesters are not sex-crazed perverts loose on our streets! Male pedophiles account for less than 1 percent of the adult male population (Langevin, 1989). Over 92 percent of child abuse cases, including same-gender abuse, involve heterosexuals, not homosexuals (Blumenfeld & Raymond, 1988).

Research and the opinions of those who actually work with molestation cases agree that there is *no* connection between pedophilia and homosexuality. That does not mean that some homosexuals are not pedophiles. But the overwhelming majority of pedophiles are heterosexual men. In spite of the obvious evidence to the contrary, the Christian right continues to perpetrate the myth that homosexuality equals pedophilia.

"Child molestation and the homosexual movement" was the title of an article Steve Baldwin contributed to *Whistleblower* magazine. Joseph Farah, another contributing writer, wrote an article in the same edition, entitled **"Activists in the newsroom."** In the article, Farah contends that many homosexuals have risen to powerful positions in the mainstream media and they make it almost *impossible* to present the heterosexual perspective of news stories. What? Is there *any* evidence to support that statement?

I have worked in several TV newsrooms as a feature TV reporter and I have worked at radio stations in New Orleans, Philadelphia, Miami, Denver, San Diego, Seattle, and Portland, Oregon. In the thirty-three years I have been in the business there has not been one incident when special consideration was given to a gay topic at the expense of the heterosexual perspective. Not one!

So how could *Whistleblower* magazine print a story that is so misleading? There is no evidence writer Joseph Farah could uncover that would support his false claim. But those who read a publication like *Whistleblower* magazine actual*ly want* to believe the accusation that the "liberal" news media give special treatment to gay news stories. But that is not true.

The American Academy of Pediatrics endorsed homosexual adoption in 2002. This credible group is much more knowledgeable on the topic than writers like Steve Baldwin and Joseph Farah. The group of pediatrics finds that gay couples can provide the healthy families children need. **The American Academy of Child and Adolescent Psychiatry** and the **American Psychological Association** are two prestigious organizations that also support homosexual adoption.

The American Academy of Pediatrics went so far as to urge its 55,000 members to actively support laws that make homosexual adoption legal. **The Academy** said of its policy, *"there is no basis on which to assume that a parental homosexual orientation will increase likelihood of or induce homosexual orientation in the child."* But the Reverend Louis Sheldon, chairman of the **Traditional Values Coalition**, a Christian group, wants you to believe that he is more knowledgeable about children than the **American Academy of Pediatrics.**

In an article on the CBSNews.com Web site, the Reverend Sheldon accused the Academy of being a *"group of pro-homosexual people…who want to further tear down the one-man, one-woman relationship in America."* That statement is simply one man's bias opinion, which is not supported by facts. Maybe someone should "blow the whistle" on the inaccuracies of *Whistleblower* magazine?

On the op/ed page of the *Detroit Free Press* was an editorial on gay adoption. Here is an excerpt from the editorial, which appeared on February 5, 2002:

> *"Denying legal parent status through adoption… prevents [children] from enjoying the psychological and legal security that comes from having two willing, capable and loving parents."*

In support of gay adoption, the editorial pointed out that there is a lack of information indicating any harmful effects to children who are raised by gay or lesbian parents.

Adopt a Special Kid is a nonprofit group based in Oakland, California, which handles adoptions for toddlers and teenagers. Family coordinator for the group, Andrea Schneider said, *"I actively seek gay and lesbian families."* She believes that gay and lesbian families have a strong sense of community and consistently more supportive friends. Based on my life experiences, I would have to agree.

A Census Bureau report released on August 22, 2003 indicated that 78 percent of all adopted children live in two-parent, married couple households. An article in the *Rocky Mountain News* in Denver reported that *"as many as 14 million children in the United States are being raised by at least one parent who is homosexual."* But homosexual parents were raising children many years before this became a controversial issue and there is no evidence suggesting that those children have suffered in any negative way as a result of being raised by a homosexual parent.

That being the case, why is the Christian right promoting the fear that children who are raised in a household with one or two homosexual parents will face hardships and behavioral problems? The rhetoric of the conservative Christian right is based entirely on their disapproval of the private sex lives of law-abiding citizens who are gay or lesbian.

Only 5 to 10 percent of the U.S. population is homosexual and according to a survey in *Demography* magazine, 95 percent of partnered gay males and 78 percent of lesbian-partnered households do not have children living with them. The percentage of gay males and lesbians raising adopted children is so miniscule that even those arguing against gay adoption could not logically believe that such adoptions would have any adverse effect on America's respect for marriage or families.

There are many more children in need of loving, caring parents and less loving, caring parents to go around. The specific sexual activity two consenting adults engage in should be private, be it homosexual or heterosexual. It is appropriate to explain the "facts of life" in an honest way when it is deemed a child is ready for the information. But the specifics of the erotic aspect of sexual activity should not be something a child is exposed to in any household, straight or gay. Children in heterosexual households are not generally exposed to graphic details concerning their heterosexual parents' sex lives. And there is no reason to believe that it would be any different for a child growing up with responsible homosexual parents.

Sexual orientation, which should be a private matter, is not a legitimate reason to disqualify an individual or a couple from adopting a child in need of a permanent parent and a secure home. Too many credible organizations have found there are no legitimate reasons to oppose gay and lesbian adoption. It's time to stop giving credit to those who want the government to control the type of sexual activity consenting adults can engage in.

The physical nature of gay and lesbian sex defies the biology that accounts for our existence, but having children is not always the primary reason that heterosexual couples get married. Promising to bring children into the world has never been a prerequisite for marriage. The fact that same-sex couples cannot naturally, as couples, have children should never be accepted as an argument against gay marriage.

Heterosexual couples have the right to make a conscious decision not to have children, and some heterosexual couples are biologically incapable of naturally having children. Should these heterosexual couples not be allowed to marry because they will not or cannot naturally bring children into the world?

The condemnation of homosexual adoption comes from many heterosexual Christian couples that are not willing to adopt a child themselves. Why, then, should they oppose a gay individual or a gay couple from providing the home they are not willing to provide?

Non-stop news

In April of 2004 there were news stories every day about the battle over gay marriage. Gay marriage had become the new social issue for the conservatives during the election of 2004. Even though George W. Bush's opponent, Democratic Senator John Kerry, also opposed gay marriage, the Bush-Cheney Re-election Committee believed the majority of voters opposed to gay marriage the would perceive President Bush as the one who would maintain a stronger conviction in the fight against gay marriage.

The Mayor of San Francisco, Gavin Newsom, began issuing marriage licenses to same-sex couples based on the assumption that there was no specific wording in the state's constitution and no city ordinance prohibiting same-sex marriage. However, the issuing of marriage licenses to same-sex couples was halted by the courts, but not before thousands of gays and lesbians had received marriage licenses.

On August 12, 2004, the California Supreme Court ruled that the almost 4,000 same-sex marriages sanctioned in San Francisco were immediately nullified. But the court stopped short of defining marriage. The ruling simply stated that San Francisco Mayor

Newsom superseded his authority by allowing marriage licenses to be issued to same-sex couples.

Del Martin, 83, and Phylis Lyon, 79, became the first same-sex couple to be married in San Francisco. In and article in *The USA Today* Phylis Lyon was quoted saying, *"After being together for mane than 50 years, it is a terrible blow to have the rights and protections of marriage taken away from us. At our age, we do not have the luxury of time."* What right do others have to rob Del and Phylis of the opportunity to express their love for each other through the bond of legal marriage? That doesn't seem very Christian-like to me. And how could the marriage of an 83-year-old lesbian to her 79-year-old lover cause any harm in our society? Their marriage was nullified.

In Portland, Oregon, a number of gays and lesbians got married until the court put a temporary end to same-sex marriages. The mayors of small towns in New York and New Mexico allowed gay couples to legally marry, but both were stopped shortly after the process became public.

It didn't take President Bush long before he officially announced his support of a constitutional amendment prohibiting gay marriage. The battle over gay marriage still raged in Massachusetts, where at the end of March 2004, lawmakers in the state were still hoping to pass a state constitutional amendment banning same-sex marriage. The lawmakers did, however, approve "legal civil unions" for homosexuals. The Massachusetts state Supreme Court set May 17, 2004 as the first day marriage licenses could be issued to same-sex couples, but another court decision put that date on hold.

The state of Maryland's house of delegates approved a bill that would give same-sex couples the opportunity to register as "life partners," which meant homosexual partners would have the right to make medical decisions concerning their partners.

Also during the last week of March 2004, the American Civil Liberties Union filed a lawsuit against the state of Washington on behalf of eleven same-sex couples. The suit challenged the Washington state constitution by claiming there was no specific wording that *prohibited* gay marriage.

On May 18, 2004, the day following the issuance of legal marriage licenses to gay and lesbian couples in Massachusetts,

Ohio Secretary of State Kenneth Blackwell joined the **Conservative Family Research Council** and Republican Representative Marilyn Musgrave of Colorado at a press conference in Washington, D.C. to announce that Congress must act rapidly to pass a constitutional amendment that would ban same-sex marriages. Blackwell said that gay marriage would lead to destructive consequences in America. Trust that in the future, Blackwell, Musgrave, the **Conservative Family Research Council**, and many others will never admit that their predictions of societal devastation were proven to be wrong.

Even heterosexuals who find gay sex to be repulsive must be aware of the dangerous waters in which they want America to tread. Asking the government to make a legal decision concerning which citizens are free to choose their companion for life, or until divorce, sets a frightening precedent.

As the day gay marriage was to become legal in the state of Massachusetts approached, America's collective opinion on the issue was already beginning to shift. A *USA Today*/CNN/Gallup public opinion poll published in *USA Today* on May 18, 2004—the day after same-sex marriage licenses were issued—showed that in December 2003, 31 percent of the adults surveyed believed that gay marriage should be legal. By May 4, 2004—almost two weeks *before* marriage licenses would be issued in Massachusetts—support for gay marriage had risen to 42 percent! And that was just the beginning of the change in attitudes towards gay marriage.

In a CBS News poll released on May 31, 2004, support for same-sex marriage had grown slightly from a poll taken several months prior. Should same-sex couples be allowed to legally marry? Twenty-eight percent of those surveyed approved of same-sex marriage becoming legal compared to 22 percent in March 2004.

Support for civil unions increased from 22 percent to 29 percent over the same period. But a majority of Americans, 60 percent, favored a constitutional amendment that would define marriage as a union between a man and a woman only.

The CBS News poll released on May 31, 2004 provided an indisputable indication that while a majority of Americans opposed gay marriage, an overwhelming majority did not believe the gay marriage issue should be part of the campaign. Seventy percent responded that they *did not* want the issue of same-sex marriage to be part of the campaign. That was up from 65 percent just three months earlier.

By the end of May 2004, there was already compelling evidence that a majority of Americans may have opposed legal gay marriage on a personal level, but rejected the idea of government involvement in personal decisions. Gay marriage as a political issue will fade.

As I predicted earlier, the political attitude among Americans towards same-sex marriage will change in the same way political attitudes changed towards the abortion issue. During the election campaigning of 2004, President Bush used his stance on the gay marriage issue to rally the support of his religious conservative base. Bush also carefully used words to remind voters that his religious beliefs would always be used to guide his policies.

The results from Election Day 2004 indicated that voters in America were not ready to embrace the idea of gay marriage. In November 2004, voters in eleven states approved constitutional amendments prohibiting same-sex marriage.

Below are the results from the states that approved a ban on same-sex marriage:

Arkansas	75% to 25%
Georgia	77% to 23%
Kentucky	75% to 25%
Michigan*	59% to 41%
Mississippi	86% to 14%
Montana	66% to 34%
North Dakota	73% to 27%
Ohio	62% to 38%
Oklahoma	76% to 24%
Oregon*	57% to 43%
Utah	66% to 34%

*Michigan and Oregon, the two states that might be described as the more **progressive thinking** states among the states that approved an amendment banning gay marriage, registered the closest margin. In the rest of the states the margin of victory was much wider. The Southern states, along with North Dakota and Oklahoma had the biggest wins for the ban on same-sex marriage. Speaking honestly, all of those states would be considered the more traditional minded states. **Backward thinking** might be another way to put it!

Tempting as it might be for the conservative Christian right, no conclusions can be drawn from the lopsided results from 2004 on state constitutional amendments prohibiting gay marriage. The very fact that a vote on these amendments was approved for the ballots indicates how the majority of voters in those states felt about the issue even before the election.

The possible debate over opposite sex-marriage

Thousands and thousands of years ago, there must have been a time when there was a divisive debate over marriage-*heterosexual* marriage! That debate would have centered on whether people should be allowed to select a partner for life. After all, humans were born with the sexual instincts to have *more* than one partner.

Could the argument not have been made that "marriage" between *one* man and *one* woman denies men and women of the natural human desire and instinct to have more than one sex partner? At the time, wouldn't *opposite*-sex marriage have been considered unnatural and contrary to tradition? That is a major part of today's argument against gay marriage.

Does that mean a homosexual choosing a partner for life is more unnatural than a heterosexual's desire to mate with more than one human? The definitions of "natural" and "traditional" are defined in the context of the times.

PART II

Chapter 3:

Does God Love Homosexuals, Too?

If Jesus were selecting his disciples today, how do we know He wouldn't choose a couple of women and a homosexual? Were not the disciples reflective of the social and political times of two thousand years ago? Then wouldn't it be reasonable to assume that a selection of disciples today would reflect the current status of women and homosexuals compared to that of the past?

The battle over gay marriage is being waged on several fronts, but it is the religious condemnation of homosexuality that has injected the most passion into the controversy. The consecration of an openly gay bishop by the Episcopal Church in November of 2003 was one of the key battles that carried the debate into 2004.

The Reverend Vickie Gene Robinson (a male) was consecrated as the first openly gay bishop in the Episcopal Church in a ceremony in Robinson's diocese of Durham, New Hampshire. A woman from the diocese said that the consecration of a gay bishop will send the Episcopal Church into unrighteousness and will break God's heart. Bishop David Bena of Albany, New York said he and many Episcopal and Anglican leaders refused to recognize the new gay bishop. The American Anglican Council immediately began accepting applications from congregations that wanted to be led by conservative bishops who denounced homosexuality.

The Anglican Church of Nigeria immediately broke off all relations with the U.S. Episcopal Church over the consecration of Bishop Robinson. Nigerian Archbishop Peter Akinola said his church would not recognize Bishop Robinson and would boycott all meetings attended by the Episcopal Church. Archbishop Akinola said the consecration of a gay bishop was a satanic attack on the Church.

The consecration of Bishop Robinson had real consequences, since it gave the perception of religious acceptance of homosexuality by a historic and traditional church. The Episcopal Church came into existence when the Church of England spread through the British Empire. The Episcopal Church is the American branch of the Anglican Communion, which holds over 2,000 years of catholic and apostolic tradition going back to Christ himself. The Archbishop of Canterbury is the spiritual leader of the Anglican Communion. Former Archbishop of Canterbury George Carey declared that the consecration of an openly gay Episcopal bishop had caused *"incalculable"* damage to the world's Anglican Communion.

In a letter to the *Times of London* newspaper, Carey said he shared the "principled distress" of Anglicans denouncing the consecration of Bishop Robinson. The former archbishop said the damage caused by this consecration to *"ecumenical relations, interfaith dialogue and the mission of the worldwide church are incalculable."* Carey was archbishop of Canterbury and spiritual leader of the world's Anglicans from 1991 to 2002. He presided over a 1998 conference that denounced homosexuality as incompatible with scripture.

On Sunday, November 9, 2003, the new bishop of New Hampshire began his ministry as the first openly gay priest in the Episcopal Church. Bishop Robinson said he wanted to bring the message of God to *"those on the margins."* He said those who are upset with his consecration should remain within the denomination.

On that Sunday in November, Episcopalians opposed to the consecration of a gay bishop walked out of their church's service in Rochester, New Hampshire. Other worshipers at the Church of the Redeemer were angry that New Hampshire's outgoing bishop, Douglas Theuner, dismissed their pastor, the Reverend Donald Wilson. Bishop Theurner ousted the Reverend Wilson because

Wilson said he would not be loyal to the new bishop because of a *"greater loyalty to our Lord."* Almost half of the members of the Episcopal Parish in Rochester walked out of the church service on that Sunday in protest of the dismissal of their minister who opposed the new gay bishop.

The Episcopal diocese of Pittsburgh amended its constitution because of the consecration of a gay bishop. An Episcopal priest called the consecration *"heresy."* The new amendment declared the church's acceptance of a gay bishop as action that is *"contrary to the historic faith and order"* of the Episcopal Church. Leaders of the diocese in Pittsburgh had previously passed a resolution denouncing Bishop Theurner and any recognition of the blessing of same-sex unions.

On Sunday, November 30, 2003, an Episcopal church in a suburb of Pittsburgh made a statement that many Episcopalians were serious about their contempt for the church's first openly gay bishop. That Sunday, St. Paul's reported that attendance was down by 100 and their annual pledges were off by $125,000. Bishop Robert Duncan of Pittsburgh had been breaking off ties with the Episcopal Church over the consecration of Bishop Robinson. But St. Paul's Church wanted to continue its connection with the Church. Officials of the parish said that members of St. Paul's were disappointed over maintaining a relationship with the Church. Bishop Duncan made the point that the Episcopal Church had not changed, rather some members of the church had *"stepped out of bounds and we're trying to put pressure on them to come back."*

Reaction to the consecration of the openly gay Bishop Robinson was immediate, demonstrating that the opposition of a major religion's acceptance of homosexuality was fierce and definite. By December of 2003, the division of the Episcopal Church had already begun.

Conservative members of the Church who opposed the promotion of an openly gay priest were building a network of churches under the leadership of Bishop Duncan of Pittsburgh. The American Anglican Council announced that thirteen conservative Episcopal bishops were ready to guide the new, separate congregations. An official request was made to have the Archbishop of Canterbury, Rowan Williams, lead the new direction.

Presiding Bishop Frank Griswold tried to discount the internal divisiveness over the consecration of Bishop Robinson. Bishop Griswold sent a letter to all of the American bishops, which promised a plan to provide alternative leadership for those congregations wishing to separate from the rest of the Church.

As the calendar turned to 2004, a Church of Uganda official said the Episcopal Church's *"faithful bishops, opposed to gays"* were invited to attend the consecration ceremony of Bishop Henry Orombi. But those Episcopalians who supported the newly consecrated gay bishop were not welcome.

The continuing battle over the acceptance of homosexuality in the Episcopal Church is a microcosm of the resistance homosexuals face in every aspect of society. Many in the Episcopal Church will not recognize the new bishop, but the fact that he was consecrated will prove to be more powerful than opposition to the gay bishop.

An overwhelming majority of those who oppose homosexuality do so on religious grounds. Scriptures from the Bible are used over and over to condemn the homosexual lifestyle in the name of God.

How to use the Bible in the debate over gay rights

Do the religious zealots who repeatedly use **Leviticus 18:22**, which does label homosexuality an "abomination," realize that **Leviticus 11:10** condemns the eating of all shellfish? Do those who use the Bible to condemn homosexuality know that **Leviticus 25:44** states that it is okay for followers of the Bible to own slaves, male and female, if they are purchased from neighboring states? **Leviticus** gives Americans permission to *own* Canadians or Mexicans.

How can homosexuality be condemned by Biblical scripture when **Exodus 35:2** sentences those who work on the Sabbath to death? **Exodus 21:7** approves of daughters being sold into slavery. **Leviticus 15:19-24** states that a man is not to have any contact with a woman during her period. Regardless of the tenacity with which Christians use the Bible to condemn homosexuality, there is *more* scripture that rebuts their judgment.

If **Leviticus 18:12** is used to condemn homosexuality in the name of God, then why should other parts of **Leviticus** not be considered applicable in today's world? If the Bible is to be taken literally, then the entire Bible should be taken literally and not just those sections that can be used support a specific religious and political agenda.

Literally translating the Bible to conveniently support the contention that homosexuality is inherently and morally wrong is flawed. There is danger in that approach! Literal translation of the Bible could lead to the condemnation of Jesus' parents, Mary and Joseph, for child endangerment!

In the second chapter of **Luke**, there is the story of Jesus' parents taking their son—the Son of God—to the annual festival of the Passover in Jerusalem. Mary, Joseph, Jesus, and the group of travelers who accompanied them to the festival started to return home and *assumed* Jesus was with the group. Twelve-year-old Jesus remained behind. After a full day of traveling, they noticed that Jesus was not with them. Mary and Joseph quickly returned to Jerusalem to search for their son.

After three days of searching, Mary and Joseph found their twelve-year-old son in the temple, listening to the teachers and asking them questions. When his parents did find him, they were shocked, and Mary said, *"Child, why have you treated us like this? Your father and I have been searching for you in great anxiety."* Jesus replied to his mother, *"Why were you searching for me? Did you not know I would be in my Father's house?"* Good answer! Jesus' parents traveled for an entire day before they realized that their son—at the age of twelve—was missing? In today's world, Child Protective Services would have been all over that!

If the Bible is to be literally translated to condemn homosexuality, then the Bible could also be used to charge Jesus' parents with neglect and child endangerment. There could have been tragic consequences from leaving a twelve-year-old boy behind. Had something tragic happened to Jesus when He was left behind, the prophecy of the Bible might not have been fulfilled and Mel Gibson would not have been able to make *The Passion of the Christ.*

This Biblical story about Mary and Joseph leaving Jesus in Jerusalem demonstrates how the Christian right selectively uses the Bible to support their anti-gay agenda, while ignoring significant parts of the Bible that do not support their agenda.

The consecration of Bishop V. Gene Robinson by the Episcopal Church was a very early sign of religious acceptance of homosexuality.

Most organized religions are not openly accepting of homosexuality; however, the Episcopal Church has set a strong example for the further inclusion of homosexuals into congregations.

An openly gay priest in the Episcopal Church represents one victory in the battle over equal rights for gays, but the truly significant battles lie on the horizon.

The states of Vermont and Hawaii have been the frontrunners in the attempt to legalize same-sex marriages. With the state's Supreme Court ruling, Massachusetts became another state getting closer to recognizing legal gay marriage. A few places in Canada are now allowing same-sex marriages to be performed and those marriages have been officially recognized. And this is just the beginning.

Republicans on Capitol Hill will lead the attempts to pass legislation banning same-sex marriage. The greatest opposition to same-sex marriage comes from political conservatives, yet they are oblivious to their own hypocrisy. Conservative ideology is based, in part, on the power of the individual to make decisions without government intervention. Conservatives opposed to gay sex or gay marriage defy their own ideology by asking the government to pass legislation that would dictate the personal, private behavior of individual citizens.

The problem with many conservatives—and I realize I'm generalizing—is that they feel the need to tell others how to lead their lives, whether it is gays and lesbians, or women who choose to have a legal abortion. Individuals have a right to follow the instincts that are congruent with their own inner guiding light-not the guiding light of someone else.

"If a man (or woman) does not keep pace with his companions, perhaps it is because he (or she) hears a different drummer."
Henry David Thoreau

As a radio talk show host, I had many discussions on the air about the controversy over gay marriage. Never did the discussion about allowing homosexuals to marry fail to include people calling and asking, *"What's next, fathers marrying their daughters, pedophiles marrying children, or men marrying their dogs?"* I always asked those individuals to explain the difference between two consenting adults having sex and a pedophile marrying a child or a man marrying his dog. The answer seemed obvious to me, but that obvious answer consistently eluded those blinded by their myopic agenda and narrow religious beliefs.

The fact that those who condemn homosexuality cannot distinguish between consenting adults enjoying a natural sexual activity inspired by their instincts and a man marrying his dog or a father marrying his daughter is but another indication that the resistance to accept homosexuality as a normal functioning part of life is void of logic.

Consenting adults agreeing to have sex bares no comparison to a man marrying his dog or a father marrying his daughter. This is the incredibly obvious difference-**dogs** and **daughters** cannot give reasonable consent. What's so difficult to understand about that?

Those on the far right of the political spectrum want to use politicians and the government to stop individuals from a lifestyle *they* believe is morally wrong. Another argument I always heard when discussing gay rights on talk radio was that America was founded on Judeo-Christian values and those values oppose homosexuality.

Let me set the record straight on the idea that America was founded on Judeo-Christian values. Much to the surprise of many Christian Americans this country was *not* founded on Judeo-Christian values. It is true that the predominant religion of those who helped start this new country was Christianity, but one of the most fundamental rights that was to be granted in the New World was the freedom to pursue religious beliefs free from government intervention. **Freedom of religion** superseded the fact that Christianity was the predominant religion when America was conceived. America was founded on freedom of religion, *not* Christian values. This truth cannot be ignored.

The judgment of homosexuality among conservative Christians is selective. Many Christians who *condemn* homosexuality on religious grounds are willing to *accept* those who have been divorced. Would anti-gay Christians who have been divorced condemn themselves with the vigor they denounce homosexuals? The Bible condemns divorce. Choosing which groups are to be condemned to hell, while other groups are forgiven, is blatant religious hypocrisy!

If the homosexual lifestyle is a sin in the hearts and minds of many Christians and Jews, then why are the teachings of Jesus so easily tossed along the way? The same group that condemns homosexuality on religious grounds accepts sinners, like those who have broken the bond of marriage. What makes one sin so different from another sin when neither sin claims an innocent victim? I am using the word "sin," in this case, to reflect the beliefs of the Christian right and not my own belief that homosexuality is a sin.

Separation of church...and homosexuality

The opposition to granting all rights to homosexuals and the blatant criticism of homosexual behavior are fundamentally grounded in religious beliefs. To use one's religious beliefs as the basis for supporting government intervention in the private lives of individuals is equal to tearing down the sacred curtain that separates church and state.

The distinction between religion and government was part of the early history of America nearly 100 years *before* the Constitution was even written. It is true that there is no actual wording in the Constitution that specifies separation of religion and government; but the use of the word "religion" in the First Amendment is synonymous with the phrase, "separation of church and state."

It was James Madison who first applied the concept of separation between religion and government. Thomas Jefferson wrote the "Bill for the Establishment of Religious Freedom," which became law in 1786. More than ten years after the First Amendment was ratified, then-president Thomas Jefferson used the phrase *"separation of church and state."*

Replying to a letter from the Baptists of Connecticut on January 1, 1802, Jefferson wrote, *"I contemplate with sovereign reverence that act of the whole American people which declared that there legislature should make no law respecting an establishment of religion, or prohibiting the free exercise thereof: thus building a wall between church and state."*

Jefferson's writing clearly established the intent of separation of church and state. Our Founding Fathers sought to create a definite distinction between religion and government. The concept of separation of church and state was passed on from generation to generation and has become a generally accepted part of American society.

The Religious Right attaches much of its agenda to the concept that America's Founding Fathers were overwhelmingly Christian. But those Christian Founding Fathers established the idea that Christians—as well as any other religious group—should not be allowed to force their religious beliefs on others-even in modern times.

The Reverend Jerry Falwell has been promoting a **Federal Marriage Amendment.** Falwell claims that granting total equality to gay Americans threatens the future of our republic and the future of Christianity. That absurd belief should automatically bring into question *anything* Falwell says, but millions of Christians share his outrageous beliefs.

In July 2003, the Reverend Falwell issued a statement that read, in part, *"we must aggressively combat the homosexual effort to destroy the tradition of marriage."* The statement also said, *"This nation is on the precipice of moral devastation."* Does the Reverend Falwell believe that gay marriage will actually lead to *"moral devastation,"* or is he attempting to frighten Americans into joining the crusade to condemn homosexuality on religious grounds?

If gay marriage were legal, some of the gay males and lesbians currently living together would get married. The day gay marriage becomes reality gays and lesbians who meet and fall in love will have the option of getting married. How could that possibly lead to "moral devastation" in America?

Legalizing gay marriage in America will not suddenly cause people to become gay. If gays are allowed to marry they will not suddenly start having sex with their new spouses on the front lawn or in public places. It is astounding that so many people have this concept of a social manifestation of gay marriage. Like the Bible, the Constitution can be very selectively interpreted to conveniently fit the malicious agenda of most any group.

The use of religious beliefs to condemn gay marriage and gay behavior violates the longstanding belief that our government should not allow a specific religion to guide the creation, execution, or interpretation of our laws. Support for the passage of federal or state laws, which would declare same-sex marriage illegal is an open invitation to request that the government create religious-based rules guiding the private lives of individuals.

Yet, those who are so passionately opposed to further acceptance of homosexuality fail to recognize that their religious beliefs are an intrusion into the personal lives of others. Ironically, the viciousness with which the Religious Right attack homosexuality defies the fundamental tenet of Christianity-do not judge others, *"lest thee be judged."*

The door leading to legislation prohibiting gay marriage is the same door that leads to the government prohibiting many other actions based on religious grounds. Is that a door we really wish to open?

The debate over same-sex marriage reflects the deep division in America that continued after the re-election of President Bush. It has also been one of the most divisive topics on talk radio across the country. In every discussion I have had on that topic, listeners have condemned same-sex marriage with grand predictions of the devastation it will cause. Yet I have not heard one reasonable argument against same-sex marriage that could not be easily refuted.

Here is a list of frequently mentioned arguments against gay marriage, followed by an easy rebuttal:

*God created males and females to physically fit together.

Rebuttal: If that's an argument against gay marriage, then it could easily be argued that God did not create male and female sex organs to be used for oral or anal sex, two sexual activities enjoyed by heterosexuals.

*God created men and women to engage in sex for the purpose of procreation.

Rebuttal: God also created people who are biologically incapable of naturally procreating. God gave people the free will to make a conscious decision *not* to bring children into the world.

*Gay sex is repulsive.

Rebuttal: Truth be known, many, and I mean many heterosexuals participate in sexual activity which is physically identical to gay sex.

*Why can't gays and lesbians be satisfied to have civil unions?

Rebuttal: The desire homosexuals have to get married is based more on love than equal benefits. If you are a married heterosexual, why did you get married? Did you marry your spouse because of the legal and financial benefits or because you were in love?

Does God *punish* those who accept homosexuals?

During the hurricane season of 2003, an act of God revealed religious broadcaster Pat Robertson to be a malicious, but passive, hypocrite. Pat Robertson has been critical of Disney World in Orlando, Florida for its annual Gay Days Festival at the theme park. The Reverend Robertson went so far as the say that God would direct hurricanes, tornadoes, and other natural disasters to strike the state of Florida as punishment for Disney World's acceptance of homosexuals.

A few years later, during the hurricane season of 2003, a strong hurricane was taking aim on North Carolina, the state where Robertson's ministry is based. As the storm continued on its path towards North Carolina Pat Robertson went public and asked all Christians to join him in praying to God that the hurricane would turn away from North Carolina. But in spite of the prayers, the hurricane did hit the state.

According to Pat Robertson, hurricanes are God's way of punishing the state of Florida for Gay Days at Disney World. If, by his own belief, a hurricane is a form of punishment, then it could be assumed that God might have been trying to punish the state of North Carolina for being the home of Pat Robertson's ministry! Could God have been trying to punish Robertson for his condemnation of homosexuality?

On January 2, 2004, Pat Robertson announced that God had spoken to him and told him that the Election of 2004 would be a "blow-out" for George W. Bush. Robertson also said that God had blessed President Bush, and even if Bush made mistakes, God would grant him victory in the presidential election of 2004. Did God lie to Pat Robertson? Or did Robertson concoct a story about God talking to him in order to make it appear that God is a Republican?

The election of 2004 was very close!

Bush (R)..........59,017,382   51%   279 electoral votes
Kerry (D)......... 55,435,808   48%   252 electoral votes

In the context of all the presidential elections America has had in modern times, the 2004 election between George W. Bush and John Kerry was close. It was not the "blow out" Robertson said God had predicted.

Robertson's motive was to place the thought in every voter's mind that voting for President Bush was a way of pleasing God. And furthermore, do you realize that Pat Robertson reduced God to a political pundit?

There was another religious broadcaster who said God spoke to him. It was Oral Roberts who said Jesus appeared as a 900-foot figure and told him that if he did not succeed in adding a new building to his religious college campus in Tulsa, Oklahoma, God would call him home. In other words, kill him! Roberts used this message from a 900-foot Jesus to con his followers out of donations to finance a new building. He was essentially saying to his followers that if they didn't send him money for the new building, God would kill him!

Well, Oral Roberts never did get enough money donated for the new building, and as I write this, he is still alive. One of two things must have happened. Either the 900-foot Jesus lied to Oral Roberts or Oral Roberts lied about God talking to him for the sole purpose of getting money from his followers.

It is so easy to discredit these religious leaders; one has to wonder why anyone would pay attention to their convictions that homosexuality is wrong in the eyes of God. And to date, Disney World has continued to support Gay Days and has yet to experience the wrath of God.

"The American family will completely fall apart" was the warning from the Reverend Ted Haggard, president of the National Association of Evangelicals, at a rally in Colorado Springs, Colorado on May 24, 2004! The rally was broadcast via satellite to churches nationwide. James Dobson, founder of Focus on the Family, was among the Christian leaders who predicted that legal gay marriage

would deprive children of the mother and father they need growing up.

Dobson announced that the Federal Marriage Amendment is only supported by thirty of the sixty-seven senators needed for passage. Dobson and Haggard pleaded with Christians to call Congress and demand that the amendment banning gay marriage be passed.

In a perfect world, every child would have a loving and caring mother and father, but God did not create a perfect world. Would James Dobson blame God for divorce, which would leave a child without both parents? These Christian evangelicals use fear as a tactic in gathering and keeping the flock that provides the money for their lavish existence. Dobson, Haggard, and the rest attempt to instill fear in people without explaining *how* gay marriage will destroy the American family and the lives of children. If challenged, these religious leaders will simply say that the Bible says homosexuality is wrong.

At the rally in Colorado Springs, Bishop Wellington Boone, a black evangelical, said that the battle over gay marriage is not a civil rights battle because he cannot *"become white,"* and many people claim to have converted from being homosexual to becoming heterosexual. There are extreme exceptions to everything in life and some people do feel as if they have consciously *become* heterosexual. If these cases are real, they are very rare. And before Bishop Boone says he can't *"become white,"* he'd better take a look at Michael Jackson!

From sex with boys to condemning gays!

Fearing that the movement to legalizing gay marriage was gaining momentum, the Catholic Church quickly responded in November 2003. The U.S. Conference of Catholic Bishops approved a statement opposing the legalization of gay marriage in America. The vote itself reflected how united the effort was against any attempt to allow legal gay marriage. By a vote of 234 to 3, with 3 abstentions, the conference of bishops approved an official stance on the issue of gay marriage. The Catholic Bishops also opposed gay couples having the right to commit themselves to their partners and to receive legal and economic benefits granted to married couples.

The statement from the bishops read, in part:

> *"To uphold God's intent for marriage, in which sexual relations have their proper and exclusive place, is not to offend the dignity of homosexual persons. Christians must give witness to the whole moral discussion against homosexual persons."*

I wonder why the bishops didn't issue a similar statement at the forefront of the sex scandal involving priests? That statement might have read:

> *"To uphold God's intent for celibate priests, in which sexual relations with young boys have their proper and exclusive place, is not to offend the dignity of those persons who deem it wrong. Christians must give witness to the whole moral discussion against pedophile priests."*

The statement on homosexuality and marriage from the Conference of Catholic Bishops also said, "Truths about marriage are present in the order of nature and can be perceived by the light of human reason. They have been confirmed by divine Revelation in Sacred Scripture."

To his credit, Bishop Wilton Gregory, president of the bishops' conference, did point out that many would question the Catholic Church's stance on the morality of gay marriage in the wake of the sex scandal involving priests molesting children. Bishop Gregory said, "The Church is human, but she must be run by the passion and the prophetic office given her by Christ."

The Catholic Church was more expedient and forthright in addressing the issue of gay marriage than it was in dealing with priests who were known to be molesting young boys. To date, there has been no explanation from the Church as to why the idea of two consenting **adults** engaging in sex, or getting married, is a more prominent problem than priests using their trust and authority to lure innocent young children into their clutches for the purpose of playing with their genitals, performing oral or anal sex with the boys, or having the children watch the priests masturbate. The Catholic Church owes every Catholic, and the world, an explanation for its tolerance of molesting priests.

The Conference of Catholic Bishops does not represent all Catholics. An interfaith gay advocacy group, Soulforce, reacted to the statements about gay marriage from the Catholic bishops by saying that opposition to gay marriage is "confusing, harmful and spiritually violent." Laura Montgomery Rutt, a spokesperson for the group, said, "When will the Catholic Church learn that this kind of spirited violence leads to great pain, suffering and even death?" Gay bashing has led to deaths and the many young gays and lesbians who have committed suicide did so because they felt shunned by the society they were born into. Gays and lesbians suffer great emotional pain every day simply because of their homosexuality.

At the end of November 2003, Massachusetts' Roman Catholic bishops said their state's Supreme Court ruling establishing the right for gays to have a legal marriage was a "national tragedy." In a letter that was sent to all Catholic priests to be read at all the masses in the state on Sunday, November 30, 2003, the bishops said that marriage is a gift from God and "not just one lifestyle among many."

To describe legal marriage for same-sex couples as a "national tragedy" is to insult all the victims of real national tragedies. The term "national tragedy" should be reserved for events like the terrorist attacks of September 11, 2001, the bombing of the Federal Building in Oklahoma City, the assassination of President Kennedy in 1963, and the two NASA space shuttle disasters. Those events deserve to be on a list of "national tragedies," not same-sex marriage.

By making this comparison, these Catholic bishops have been disrespectful to every victim of the aforementioned tragedies, along with their families and friends. How can the bishops claim to be religious leaders and good Catholics if they are going to compare the deaths of over 3,000 people on September 11, 2001 to gay marriage? This can't be the view of anyone who loves and respects the God I know!

On December 16, 2003, Boston Archbishop Sean O'Malley told a meeting of about 600 Catholic priests that tolerating same-sex marriage would prove to be "a tragedy for the entire country."

O'Malley urged priests to ask their parishioners to let lawmakers know that there must be a fight to stop same-sex marriage in Massachusetts. Archbishop O'Malley said if the newly interpreted definition of marriage by the state's Supreme Court was allowed to become the law of the land, Catholics in the state "shall have to answer to God."

In a sermon on Sunday, January 11, 2004, Bishop O'Malley said, "The social cost of the breakdown of family life has already been enormous." O'Malley asked lawyers and judges to oppose gay marriage saying that marriage and the family unit are "threatened as never before." If I felt that legal gay marriage would, indeed, threaten the institution of marriage and the family, I would not have written a book that explains why heterosexuals should actively support the gay rights movement.

Will gay marriage actually threaten marriage and the family? Bishop O'Malley and others are quick to predict that gay marriage will have a negative impact on marriage and the family, but they never explain how or why it will happen.

Following the Mass with Bishop O'Malley's sermon about gay marriage, former Supreme Judicial Court Justice Joseph R. Nolan, president of the Catholic Lawyers Guild, expressed his support of O'Malley's words condemning gay marriage, and called such an institution an "abomination."

In addition, former ultra-conservative Supreme Court nominee Robert Bork condemned the Massachusetts Supreme Court ruling that the state's constitution did not contain wording prohibiting gay marriage. Bork said the ruling "justifies the term judicial tyranny." And then Bork, (thank God he never reached the Supreme Court) predicted that the U.S. Supreme Court will "go in the direction of" the Massachusetts Supreme Court and that gay marriage will become legal nationwide. A glimmer of hope spilled from the lips of an ultra-conservative codger! However, Bork's prediction was designed to strike fear in Catholics.

The new leader of Boston's Roman Catholic Archdiocese, Bishop O'Malley, was installed on July 30, 2003. O'Malley took over after Cardinal Bernard Law resigned amid the sex scandal that rocked the Catholic Church. Law admitted that for years, he protected priests he knew were having sexual relations with children. He would simply transfer the pedophile priest to another parish. Cardinal Law was actually transferring these priests to allow them to have fresh children to molest. A report on the church's sex scandal released at the end of 2003 revealed that the molestation of children by priests was continuing.

It occurs to me that Bishop O'Malley and the Catholic Church, in general, should focus on the very serious problem of priests having sex with children rather than getting involved in the private lives of consenting gay adults. Catholic priests having sexual contact with children are committing a sin that damages all of the young victims for the rest of their lives. Two consenting adults agreeing to sexual activity brings harm to no one and yet the Church has been quick to join the crusade against gay marriage while allowing serious illegal actions to occur within its protected walls.

The Catholic Church that asked lawyers and judges to do everything possible to block gay marriage is the same Catholic Church that did not ask lawyers and judges to do everything possible to prosecute priests that enjoyed molesting children.

Hypocrisy and the Church

There was another debate in the Catholic diocese prior to Easter Sunday, April 11, 2004, which further revealed the twisted hypocrisy of the Church. Archbishop Sean O'Malley questioned whether or not Democratic presidential candidate John Kerry, a Catholic, should be allowed to take communion because of his pro-choice position on abortion.

Every Sunday in every Catholic Church in America and around the world, there are Catholics that do not subscribe to every rule of the Church receiving Holy Communion. In many cases, the priests know that certain couples are practicing birth control, yet the couples are allowed to receive Holy Communion, even though the Church condemns birth control.

Furthermore, in many parishes, priests know couples that are divorced and re-married. The pope announced a few years ago that re-married Catholics are welcome to take Holy Communion *only* if they are not having sexual relations with their current spouse. The only divorced and re-married couples invited to communion are those that have had their first marriages annulled. How many millions of Catholics fall into the category of being divorced, re-married, and sexually active with their current spouse without having had their first marriage annulled? Yet all of those Catholics are receiving communion with no questions asked.

If Catholic priests are giving Holy Communion to Catholics with the knowledge that members of the congregation are not following all of the rules of the Church, then there should never have been a question about John Kerry receiving Holy Communion. Kerry went to a Catholic church that Easter Sunday during the presidential campaign of 2004 that he knew would openly offer him communion. The judgment of the Catholic Church in these matters should discredit the Church's opinion on the gay marriage issue.

I have heard a common rebuttal to my criticism of the Catholic Church: *If you don't want to follow all the rules of the Catholic Church, then go to another church.* If that were actually the Church's protocol, in America and around the world, only a few would find their way into pews of Catholic churches. Is it necessary to accept every aspect of the rules of the Catholic Church in order to deserve Holy Communion? That's a question each practicing Catholic must answer. But always remember that the Church has been selective in its judgment of others. Why can't you be selective with the Church's rules?

Consider that the hands of some priests giving out Holy Communion at churches around the country are the same hands that played with the genitals of young boys. The mortal priests of the Catholic Church are in no position to judge who is worthy of Holy Communion. During the campaign of 2004, priests were singling out pro-choice Catholics in the way they have single-out homosexuals who desire a legal marriage.

Gay Catholic activists in Chicago decided to challenge the Church's rules for receiving Holy Communion. On Pentecost Sunday, May 30, 2004, members of the gay group **Rainbow Sash** designated themselves as homosexuals by wearing rainbow-colored sashes in church. The goal of the **Rainbow Sash Alliance** was to show the Catholic Church that it should have *"a conversion of the heart"* towards homosexuality.

Chicago Cardinal Francis George warned the gay Catholics that they would be denied communion and he instructed priests throughout the archdiocese to deny communion to anyone wearing a rainbow-colored sash. Washington Cardinal Theodore McCarrick agreed with Cardinal George and banned the **Rainbow Sash** from receiving communion. However, at the Catholic Cathedral of St. Paul, Minnesota, Archbishop Harry Flynn said that **Rainbow Sash** members would be allowed to receive communion. Archbishop Flynn also said that the sacrament of communion should only be denied in "extreme" situations. Catholic priests are not always in agreement with the Vatican. That should give all Catholics permission receive Holy Communion even if they are not in agreement with all of the rules from the Vatican.

While these gay Catholic activists wanted to make their point, the respect they had for the liturgy led to no disruption of the mass. As it turned out, on that Pentecost Sunday 2004, in some Catholic Churches homosexuals were offered communion and in other churches they were denied. Those priests who did not allow members of the **Rainbow Sash** to receive Holy Communion said they would have given communion to them if only they had not designated themselves as homosexuals by wearing the sashes. Did those priests realize that if a gay Catholic removed a rainbow-colored sash, he or she would still be gay?

Considering that it is known that some Catholic priests are homosexuals and receive Holy Communion themselves, why would it be fair to deny communion to other homosexuals?

And for those hardcore Catholics who think I may be too critical of the Catholic Church, it was announced on Thursday, May 27, 2004 that former Boston Cardinal Bernard Law was appointed by the pope to a special position in the Vatican. The Cardinal, who resigned in disgrace from the diocese in Boston for protecting many priests he *knew* were molesting young children, was appointed by the pope to a position in the Vatican! That was a disgrace and further proof the Catholic Church is still failing to understand that priests guilty of molesting children should be punished by the laws of society and not protected by the laws of the church.

Cardinal Law, by all accounts, should be in prison, but like so many others, the Church has protected him. At this point, the Catholic Church should welcome homosexuals, pro-choice political candidates, and anyone who is willing to overlook its grand hypocrisy.

Each individual in America is entitled to his or her own religious beliefs, provided those beliefs do not bring harm to others. And it stops there. From the beginning of our nation individuals were to be allowed to have their own personal view of religion, therefore religion should never be used to condemn homosexuality or gay marriage.

Chapter 4

Bonding with gays-if you're <u>not</u> gay

When I walk into a bar or nightclub I know I am different, but I wonder if anyone else realizes I'm different? I never know how to interpret the looks I receive. Are they looking at me because that's a natural thing to do when a new patron walks into a crowded bar? Or are they looking at me because I'm different? Am I being accepted or are those looks projecting an attitude that I don't belong because I am different?

That's the experience I have every time I go to a gay bar or nightclub with my lesbian or cross-dressing friends. In that setting I am the one who is different. I can't help but wonder if I'm accepted or shunned. That must be the experience gays and lesbians have when they walk into a mainstream bar, nightclub, restaurant, bookstore, or just about any place dominated by mainstream, heterosexual America.

Though I always knew I was different from the patrons in a gay bar, I began to think about why I have always sensed an unexplained close bond with gays and lesbians. What was behind the comfort level I sensed while in the company of gays and lesbians knowing that I did not have the slightest curiosity about sex with men?

While I never felt the need to justify where I went or the sexual orientation of my friends, I did ponder why I was drawn to places where I knew I would never *meet* a partner, *become* a partner, or even have the opportunity to do some healthy flirting? It is fair to assume that a great percentage of people in straight or gay bars are seeking a sex partner, or at the very least, conformation of their sexual appeal. Yet, my purpose for being in a gay bar was to hang with my friends, to dance and enjoy an evening.

An initial thought came to mind about why I frequented gay and lesbian bars. The new contempt I had developed for the overt pretentiousness that was so prominent in most popular straight bars and nightclubs caused me to reject what should have been a more natural environment for a heterosexual. Like many metropolitan cities, there are popular Friday-after-work restaurants and bars in Denver. One restaurant/bar, in particular, *Cool River Cafe* was packed with pretense every Friday after work.

One of my first nights at *Cool River* was a warm summer evening. The bar was so crowded I think I broke three of the Commandments just ordering a drink! I saw an attractive tall guy in his mid-thirties wearing a turtleneck sweater that had **"VAIL"** prominently embroidered on the neck of the sweater. It was a *warm* summer evening so why was this guy wearing a turtleneck sweater? He wasn't wearing it to keep him warm. He was wearing that turtleneck sweater to let all the ladies know that he had been to Vail, Colorado, a popular, but elite ski resort. Welcome to the superficial world of heterosexuals!

I found myself moving to various vantage points to better witness the heterosexual mating ritual. I overhear men bragging or lying about their salaries, their cars, where they lived, and where they had traveled. And the men were often talking to women with silicone breasts, an abundance of makeup, big hair, and a look in their eyes comparable to the look you'd expect to see in the eyes of a female lion in heat. Ironically, I possessed many of the qualifications those women were seeking in a guy, but I never let them know it. There I was, among attractive peers and yet I felt completely out of place.

Then there was the *Purple Martini* in downtown Denver, where young, phony females knowingly go to be visually undressed by typical, horny frat boys. From one popular bar or nightclub to another, I became reluctant to place myself in an environment where someone might look at me and think that **I was one of those guys!**

The rock group Good Charlotte expressed this reality best in their song **"Boys & Girls"**:
"Girls don't like boys, girls like cars and money. Boys will laugh at girls when they're not funny."

This pretentious view of heterosexuality is common in every city in America. I did discover a few places that featured a type of music best described as brit-glam-retro rock, where a very edgy and hip twenty-to-thirty-something crowd would dance and have fun. For some unexplained reason, that group of nightclub patrons seemed void of the insincerity I had experienced elsewhere.

However, in each of those bars and nightclubs there was always a mix of straights and gays. I wondered if the presence of gays and lesbians created a different ambience or if the different ambience attracted gays and lesbians. Other than the edgy clubs, the only other places I discovered that were void of overt pretense were gay bars and clubs.

Perhaps the pretense was present in the gay bars, but I didn't sense it since my purpose for being there was different from other patrons. I wasn't there to impress or seek a potential partner. It was a wonderful sanctuary for a heterosexual guy who had grown disgusted with the overwhelming insincerity of straight bars and clubs.

Considering I'm not gay, what was the primary inspiration that made gay and lesbian bars and clubs my entertainment destination? And why did I feel an innate bond with the gay community? The answer had been with me all of my life, but I had never consciously acknowledged it...until I began writing this book.

For as long as I can remember I always felt that I was different from everyone else, no matter where I went. What made me different was deep inside and not apparent to my parents, my classmates, girlfriends, and later my two wives and my son. I knew I was very different but I thought I was the only one who knew.

Through psychiatric help I discovered that since a very early age I have suffered from a severe case of obsessive-compulsive disorder (OCD). However, when I was growing up, and even into my early adult years, no significant information about OCD existed. Any information about OCD prior to 1987 is considered inaccurate, following extensive studies at UCLA Medical Center in Los Angeles. As I was evolving as a person I hated myself for being who I was. I knew there was something terribly wrong with the way I felt and the way my mind worked. And I was absolutely convinced that no one else understood.

Being gay...or living with O.C.D.?

My father traveled a lot on business when I was young. Whenever he was out of town—which was almost every week—I felt insecure and my OCD kicked into overdrive. To ensure that my father would return home safely, I had established a certain set of clothes that I *had* to wear each day of the week he was out of town. There was a particular pair of pants and a particular shirt I would wear on Mondays Tuesdays, Wednesdays, Thursdays, and Fridays. I honestly believed that if I did not wear those certain clothes on certain days that my father would be killed while traveling and never return home. That's a hell of a burden to bear for a young kid!

I **obsessed** over my father being gone and I acted **compulsively**—thus **obsessive-compulsive disorder**. I was a young kid, but I felt my father's life depended on what clothes I wore on certain days of the week! I know that sounds ridiculous, but unless you have obsessive-compulsive disorder it is impossible to comprehend the impact it has on your life.

Until my dad called each night to let me know he had arrived in another city safely, I was an emotional wreck. I sat in a certain position on the sofa watching TV with my hands in a particular position. To this day, when I channel surf through reruns of the TV shows I watched at that point in my life, I have vivid and painful flashbacks of how OCD affected my life.

I was convinced that I was the *only* person in the entire world with a mind that worked the way mine did. I *hated* myself for feeling so different and incapable of doing anything about it.

My parents knew I wasn't normal and that something was wrong. They sent me to two different psychiatrists. Of course, at the time, psychiatrists didn't know how to diagnose OCD Both times the psychiatrists reported to my parents that they "could find nothing wrong with me." That only made the feelings of being abnormal intensify and I became more and more isolated. I was going through the motions of living life, but I was not actually living life. The torture of the obsessive-compulsive mind is only truly known by those who have OCD.

I have been married and divorced twice. I am not proud of that, but it is my reality. As I look back on both of those marriages, I now understand how my OCD played a significant role in both of the failed marriages. Neither wife knew what was wrong with me. They just knew something was wrong. So did I, but I didn't know what it was!

For unknown reasons, obsessive-compulsive disorder has a tendency to fade about the age of 18 to about 25 and that was the way it was for me. But when it returned, it returned with a vengeance. It was a struggle to live each day and by the time I was married a second time I had become *possessed* with this disorder that had stolen my life. I knew I needed psychiatric help, but I was convinced no psychiatrist, or anyone, would have the ability to understand what I was experiencing and the way my mind operated. I didn't even know how to explain it to myself.

I will never forget the moment I realized that there was a name for the way I was! Just the fact that it had a name told me that there must be other people with a brain like mine!

The manifestation of my OCD had gone from physical things, like wearing certain clothes on certain days and making sure things around the house were in certain places, to strictly mental torture.

My disorder had manifested itself in an intense desire to be **perfect**. If the smallest, most insignificant thing was not *exactly* the way I wanted it to be, my life would stop until I was convinced that I was starting over and everything would be *perfect* from that moment on. If I made the slightest mistake on the air, only noticeable to me, I would begin the mental torture of telling myself that from that moment on I was going to be perfect and would never make that mistake again. If someone told me I just had a great show, but I was obsessed with some mistake I made or something that wasn't perfect in my mind, the compliment meant absolutely nothing. I would listen to tapes of shows when I knew I was having a serious

OCD episode and I was astonished that my OCD episode was virtually unnoticeable. But I knew it was there.

At work, or at home, I would stand in the same position with my eyes focused on a certain spot and my hands in a certain position for extended periods of time as I tried to make myself have this "perfect" feeling of confidence that things would be different from that point on. I did not want my life to continue until I had conquered the objective of knowing that my life would be changed from that moment on. And this would happen countless times a day. On some days it would seem to occur thirty, forty, fifty times. On days when there were fewer episodes the duration of each could last two or three hours. This all left little time to live life!

I recall having one O.C.D. episode that lasted the entire eight-hour drive from Memphis to New Orleans. What you should know about obsessive-compulsive disorder is that the person suffering from it does not want to continue living his or her life until the episode is over. On many occasions, I thought that the only way to end those feelings would be to end my life. I didn't actually contemplate suicide, but I simply thought about how death would end the suffering.

It was 1996 and I was 45 years old. I was reading Howard Stern's second book, _Miss America_. When I hit page 92, this is what I read:

"For twenty years, I'd been in the grips of a devastating mental illness, OCD-obsessive compulsive disorder. Unknown to anyone around me, even my lovely wife, Alison, I was a slave to a series of ritualistic behaviors that made me a prisoner of my own psyche. I suffered alone, too embarrassed to talk to anyone about it. Even though I could be licked in rituals for hours at a time, I hid it from the world.

Now, for the first time ever, I will reveal the depths of my psychic hell and relate how my redemption came at the hands of a little old man in a long white coat, Dr. John Sarno. Saint Sarno, to me."

Howard Stern went on to write about his first acknowledgement that something was wrong with him, which occurred in college. Later in the chapter, Stern wrote about the more recent manifestations of his OCD, which included rituals like, reading sentences over and over, opening a book a certain way or leaving a location only at odd minutes.

Howard then revealed more rituals that developed years later.

"If I wanted to watch TV, say, Letterman's show on Channel 4, first I had to tune past Channel 4 to Channel 5 because five dominated four. Therefore, I was greater than four and I dominated David Letterman and anything I would do would be better."

Like everyone who has successfully come to terms with their OCD, Howard Stern realized that the rituals inspired by his OCD were a form of distraction from his fear of failure.

"As a defense mechanism, my brain had set up an elaborate maze of rituals that kept me from confronting my fear."

With the help of Saint Sarno, Howard Stern learned how to confront his OCD. It never really goes away, the best one can hope for is to learn how to embrace it and control it.

It wasn't until 1998 that I finally did seek professional help. I have seen several psychiatrists around the country as a result of living in different cities. The one doctor who helped me the most was Dr. James Douglas, whom I saw while living in Portland, Oregon. I always felt that in order to accomplish what I wanted to accomplish in my life I would have to rid my mind of my OCD. Dr. Douglas taught me to embrace it as an integral part of who I was as a person. He explained that if I somehow got rid of OCD, I might be destroying an important part of who I was.

At the time, I was studying Zen and when Dr. Douglas explained that my obsessive-compulsive disorder was part of me, I read something in one of my Zen books that caused me to understand what Dr. Douglas was trying to tell me. The Zen idea was simple:

> *The light that shines on us is what we like about ourselves, but the light casts a shadow. The shadow represents what we don't like about ourselves. In order to get rid of the shadow, those things we don't like about ourselves, we would have to get rid of the light, the things we like about ourselves.*

My life was changed by the reality that what I didn't like about myself was, indeed, an integral part of who I was. If I didn't have OCD, or somehow got rid of it, the course of my life may have led me in the wrong direction. Obsessive-compulsive disorder cannot be cured, only managed.

It was Christmas Eve 2003, and I was on a plane going from Denver to Portland to visit my son, his fiancée, and my girlfriend of almost eleven years. I thought about a Christmas wish I have had since I was a kid. From younger years into adulthood, I can't remember a Christmas when I didn't silently say to myself, *"All I want for Christmas is for my OCD to go away."*

Looking back, I was really asking the only power that could actually grant such a wish...God. With the help of God, and Dr. Douglas, my obsessive-compulsive disorder is now well under control.

I could go on about obsessive-compulsive disorder, but that's not the purpose of this book. What is pertinent is that my OCD has caused me feel different from the mainstream since about the age of eleven. I always knew I was different from every other student in every school I attended. I knew I was different from those I worked with at each radio station across the country. I always felt I was different from everyone else, whether in restaurants, bars or shopping malls. I *knew* I was different. The manifestation of that is a feeling of severe alienation.

As I searched for an explanation as to why I was comfortable in gay bars and clubs, it finally occurred to me. It was my obsessive-compulsive disorder! The common bond I sensed with the homosexual community was never based on sexual preference or a curiosity for same-gender sex. It was based on the fact that all of my life, I, like most homosexuals, felt *different* from the mainstream.

The gay community is bound by a shared difference from the mainstream population. Sexual orientation is the distinct difference between the homosexual community and the heterosexual community. But sexual orientation might not be the *only* reason for an individual to sense a strong, innate bond with the homosexual community.

Any heterosexual who has gone through the experience of feeling alienated from the general population, for whatever reason, shares an intrinsic bond with the gay community. For me, coming to that realization was an epiphany.

In America, Jews feel differently from the mainstream and are bound together through their common religious traditions and their history. The black community shares a common bond from their continuing battle over institutionalized racism. At the beginning of the Women's Liberation Movement in the '70s, women bonded over their quest for equal rights. But of all the groups that are bound through a particular commonality, the gay community has perhaps the strongest bond.

While no group can boast total unity, the individuals who make up the homosexual community do have a particularly powerful bond. Since our sexuality is a defining aspect of our whole being, it should not be surprising that the common bond of sexual preference is an extremely powerful one. This bond is strengthened by a collective sense of being shunned by society. If the individuals of an entire group are made to feel alienated by the mass population, it's logical that the common rejection would push the individuals of that group together.

Homosexuals, like anyone who is perceived as being "different," learn to instinctively develop a unique strength in order to deal with the unique challenges life presents. In the book, *Evolution, Culture, and Consciousness*, Professor Thomas McNamara concludes:

> *"Many homosexuals develop the emotional strength to overcome the prohibitions of childhood programming and social controls. Consequently, they achieve the freedom to make their sexual preferences known publicly. They thereby develop a lifestyle in keeping with their sexual orientation. The attainment of such a high level of emotional strength and freedom—provided it is not motivated by unhealthy desires, such as anger or rebellion—is a major spiritual achievement and a huge advance in fulfilling their higher needs. As a result of successfully meeting their need for self-expression by creating their own meanings, gay men and women can experience a much greater degree of creativity than heterosexuals who remain comfortably wrapped in society's norms."*

So that's why homosexuals are more "creative" and "open" than heterosexuals are!

I have explained my battle with obsessive-compulsive disorder and the consequential feelings of isolation from others, but there may be other reasons heterosexuals might sense a common bond with the homosexual community.

Sexual orientation is not the only reason for feeling out of sync with what seems to be the societal norm. If more heterosexuals would consider the things they *share* with the homosexual community, rather than focusing so much on the one major difference, there might have been no need to write a book about why heterosexuals should support equal rights for gays and lesbians.

Chapter 5

The Gay Agenda—What *Special* Rights?

Gays want *special* rights? The word "agenda" has come to represent the goals of aggressive, militant groups in their fight for a cause, often one not shared by the majority.

Many Americans are deeply concerned about the "gay agenda," believing it represents the goal to win *special* rights for gays. What *special* rights? In the '60s, did African Americans want *special* rights? In the '70s, did women want *special* rights? And today, do homosexuals want *special* rights? The objective of the gay agenda or gay movement or whatever you choose to call it has not been about *special* rights. As with African Americans and women, the only objective has been achieving *equal* rights.

Gay men, in particular, continue to be the targets of violent attacks simply because of their sexual orientation. The most current statistics from the government show that in 2001, there were 1,103 hate crimes on record against gay males. In the same year, 245 lesbians were the victims of hate crimes. Those figures show that a sexual relationship between two gay males is less acceptable to mainstream America than the sexual relationship between two women.

If gay males and lesbians were, in the opinion of many Christians, committing a sin by participating in homosexual sex, why would gay male couples be at greater risk?

The strongest negative reaction to gay males comes from straight males. Many of these straight males who bash gay men appear to feel threatened by the mere existence of gay men. Yet, most men will admit they are fascinated by the image of two women having sex. If homosexuality is wrong, then why are gay male couples greater targets for verbal and physical abuse?

On the afternoon of the opening of the baseball season for the Colorado Rockies, our radio talk show was on location at a popular tavern near Coors Field. Earlier in the week, we had given tickets away to listeners who were to join us at the tavern to pick up their tickets and have dinner prior to the game.

Before our talk show began, there were two gay males who listened to the show waiting to talk to me when I arrived. By coincidence, the gay rights issue was the topic on the show that day and I invited the two gay males to join us on the show with their opinions.

About thirty minutes into the show one of our listeners who had won dinner and tickets to the baseball game arrived at the remote broadcast. He had a weathered face and was wearing jeans and a baseball cap. This guy stood watching us doing the show for a few minutes before asking one of the promotion girls from the radio station for his tickets to the game. He turned down free dinner at the tavern and left immediately after receiving his tickets.

I was curious as to why the man was so anxious to leave. I asked one of the girls in charge of the promotional aspect of the broadcast why the guy asked for his tickets and departed so quickly. She told me that he wanted to pick up his tickets but not stay for the free dinner. He told the girl that he would not stay in the same bar with two "fags!" The guy had been listening and when he heard two gay guys on the show he knew they were in the bar.

I am reluctant to pass judgment based on appearance, but this macho-looking guy with the weathered face of a blue-collar worker appeared to be a stereotypical anti-gay male. He could not tolerate being in the same place with gay men. This was the type of man

97

who seemed concerned that he might "catch" homosexuality by being in the same room with gay men.

I have concluded that many straight, macho men, who would not generally be mistaken for gay males, feel as if they inherit a gay persona simply by being in the same room with gays. It's as if you go to a jukebox and push the wrong number and another song you would never want to be associated with begins playing instead. As you stand there or walk back to your table, the song you despise has suddenly become the soundtrack of your walk and your image to everyone else in the room.

The fear that others will assume a straight guy is gay because he is in the same locale with gay men is insulting to the intelligence of the entire gay *and* straight communities. The same straight macho guys who go to great lengths to avoid gay men are the same straight macho guys who would seek any opportunity to be in the presence of lesbians. Criticism of homosexuality does not fall equally on gay men and lesbians.

If homosexuality, whether male or female, were the actual reason for condemnation, then there would be no justification for a heterosexual male's desire to be in the presence of lesbians, but not gay males. It's the vision of gay male sex as a repulsive act that causes the straight man's discomfort with being around gay guys, not his disapproval of homosexuality.

I have an extremely close bond with a strikingly beautiful lesbian. After introducing her to some of the males I work with, every one of them made the comment that my real intent was to have sex with her in hopes of converting her to heterosexuality. The very thought that all a beautiful lesbian needs is to have sex with the right straight guy and she would suddenly realize she wants to be with a man is a perfect description of the inner workings of the egocentric male mind. At times, I am embarrassed to be a guy!

The other comment I often heard was that I wanted to be friends with this "lipstick" lesbian was in hopes of watching her have sex with another woman. [More on my lesbian relationship in Chapter 10]

There is another concern about being in a gay bar that is shared by many straight males. It is the fear that if a straight male walks into a gay bar, gay guys would begin "hitting on" him or grabbing his ass.

Gay males are not so desperate as to attack any male that comes into view. Perhaps these straight guys have that impression of gay men because straight guys tend to "hit on" straight women in bars and would love to grab some female ass!

My radio partner at the time, Bob Newman, is a retired marine. Bob knows that I am straight but spend a lot of time in gay, lesbian, and drag queen bars and clubs. I told Bob that he should come along the next time I hit the gay bars. I did warn Bob that there was a possibility that if he went up to the bar, the bartender might say something like, *"What can I get for you, sweetie?"* Bob did not hesitate when he said, *"I'd have to punch him!"* And he meant it!

Bob Newman is one of those straight guys who would never be comfortable in a gay bar. Bob never did go with me to a gay bar. I hesitate to label Bob, or anyone for that matter, a "homophobe." The word "homophobe" is used to describe "any heterosexual that despises homosexuals." It shouldn't be a word because the actual definition would be different. "Phobia" means fear, not hate. Regardless, the word "homophobe" has come to describe hate for homosexuals rather than a fear of them.

The story of Matthew Shepard

Homosexuals don't want special rights or special treatment; they want fair and equal treatment. Perhaps the most definitive story that demonstrates the importance of the battle for total acceptance of homosexuals is found in the sad and painfully true story of Matthew Shepard.

Matthew was a twenty-one-year old freshman at the University of Wyoming in Laramie. After attending a meeting on campus for Gay Awareness Week, Matthew went to a local bar. Two young males, Aaron McKinney, 22, and Russell Henderson, 21, approached Matthew at the bar. Matthew gave an indication that he was gay and McKinney and Henderson said they were gay, too.

According to testimony in court, McKinney and Henderson saw Matthew as an easy robbery target and lured him out of the Laramie bar and into their truck under the pretense of being gay. According to a detective in the case, McKinney said that as they drove through Laramie, Matthew put his hand on McKinney's leg. That's when McKinney revealed the truth and said, *"Guess what, we're not gay."*

The detective said that McKinney admitted hitting Matthew several times with his fist and then with the butt of a .357 magnum revolver, as Matthew begged for his life. An autopsy found that Matthew Shepard had been hit eighteen times in the head and had bruises on the backs of his hands indicating that he tried to protect himself from the attack. Matthew also suffered bruises around his groin, which meant he had been kicked in that area many times.

After savagely beating Matthew, McKinney and Henderson tied Matthew to a fencepost in a remote area outside of Laramie. Matthew Shepard was left to die in the freezing cold Wyoming weather.

In the early morning hours of October 7, 1998, after about eighteen hours of being tied to the fencepost, a bicyclist found Matthew still alive. Matthew's wrists were tied so tightly that it was difficult to cut him loose. His body was covered with blood. The only exception was one spot on his face which was clean...the clean spot was where his tears had run down his face washing away the blood.

Five days after he was rescued and hospitalized, Matthew Shepard, who never made it home on that night...did make it home-to God.

Would McKinney and Henderson have done this to just any twenty-one-year-old while robbing him of the $20 he had in his wallet? In an interview with Kristen Price, McKinney's girlfriend, she revealed that her boyfriend justified the violence by saying, *"Well, you know how I feel about gays."* During a hearing at the Albany County Courthouse in Laramie, Russell Henderson turned to Matthew's parents, Judy and Dennis Shepard, and apologized for killing their son. Russell Henderson pleaded guilty to murder to avoid being put to death. He was sentenced to two consecutive life sentences with no chance of parole. Albany County Attorney, Cal Rerucha, said, following the sentencing, *"The only time he [Henderson] leaves the Wyoming State Penitentiary is when they bury him."* Aaron McKinney was convicted of second-degree murder.

Matthew Shepard's father, Dennis, issued a statement on November 5, 1999, the day after Aaron McKinney was sentenced. Part of the statement read:

> *"My son, Matthew, paid a terrible price to open*
> *the eyes of all of us who live in Wyoming, the United*

States and the world to the unjust and unnecessary fears, discrimination and intolerance that members of the gay community face every day."

President Clinton condemned the vicious murder by saying, *"I was deeply grieved by the act of violence perpetrated against Matthew Shepard."* Clinton asked Congress to pass a Federal Hate Crimes Prevention Act, saying, *"There is nothing more important to the future of this country than our standing together against intolerance, prejudice and violent bigotry."* A statement that could have been read verbatim by President Kennedy or President Johnson regarding the Civil Rights Movement in the '60s.

Those who vehemently condemn homosexuality are the current day clones of the white people who condemned people because of their skin color in the 1950s and 1960s. This may sound harsh, but I only regret that Henderson and McKinney will probably never experience what they made Matthew Shepard endure in the closing moments of his life.

Godhatesfags.com

The Reverend Fred Phelps, pastor of the Westboro Baptist Church in Topeka, Kansas proudly maintains the Web site: *godhatesfags. com.* The Web site, among other things, keeps a daily count of what Phelps believes are the number of days Matthew Shepard has been burning in hell. Included is the following alleged quote from Matthew in hell: *"For God's sake, listen to Phelps."* At the top of one of the Web pages is a picture of Matthew Shepard with active burning flames bordering his face. I actually recommend that you go to the Web site to experience, firsthand, the hate that lives in Reverend Phelps and many others like him.

The Reverend Phelps writes:

> *"the truth about Matthew Shepard needs to be known. He lived a satanic lifestyle. He got himself killed trolling for anonymous homosexual sex in a bar at midnight. Unless he repented in the final hours of his life (not likely since God had given up on him! Romans 1), he is in hell. He will be in hell for all eternity, 'where their worm dieth not, and the*

fire is not quenched. Mark 9:44' For each day that passes, he has only eternity to look forward to. All the candlelight vigils, all the tributes, all the acts of Congress, all the rulings of the Supreme Court of the United States, will not shorten his sentence by so much as one day. And all the riches of the world will not buy him one drop of water to cool his tongue."

This so-called man of God and his followers from the Westboro Baptist Church and across the country have openly display their hatred of Matthew Shepard and all homosexuals like a religious badge of honor.

On October 12, 2002, the anniversary of Matthew's death, followers of the church held an anniversary protest celebrating Matthew Shepard's entrance into hell. The anniversary celebration took place in front of the stadium before a Colorado State football game in Ft. Collins, Colorado. Matthew died at the Poudre Valley Hospital in Ft. Collins, which is about a two-hour drive from Laramie, Wyoming.

The TV news coverage the "protest/celebration" received was disproportionate to the actual size of the protest. There were only about a dozen protesters, but their hateful **celebration** of the death of a young male homosexual made the event a magnet for TV news.

Though small in numbers, a protest inspired by a religious leader who is celebrating the anniversary of a homosexual burning in hell is so bizarre and hateful that it will attract the news media, thus giving the protesters the publicity they so desired to convey their message. However, there is a positive side to the undeserving media exposure this kind of protest receives. The news media's coverage created the opportunity for rational human beings to denounce the hate promoted by religious zealots, like Fred Phelps and his demented disciples.

One of the justifications the Reverend Phelps uses to promote hate of all homosexuals is the murder of thirteen-year-old Jesse Dirkhising from Prairie Grove, Arkansas. Two gay males sexually tortured and killed Jesse on September 26, 1998. Joshua Brown, 22, and David Don Carpenter, 38, murdered Jesse. The thirteen-year-old was found after police responded to a 911 call. Near death, Jesse was taken from the home of Brown and Carpenter and rushed to St. Mary's Hospital in Roger, Arkansas, where he died a half hour later. An investigation determined that Jesse had been raped repeatedly for hours, including with foreign objects. His ankles, knees, and wrists had been duct taped, and he was gagged, blindfolded, and tied to a mattress.

Fox News Channel's Bill O'Reilly wrote, *"The question is stark and brutal. If the murder of Matthew Shepard, a gay man, by two drunken thugs in Laramie, Wyoming, was a national story and a heinous hate crime, why wasn't the killing of 13-year-old Jesse Dirkhising publicized the same way?"* O'Reilly continued, *"The national media ignored the crime, causing outrage among those who see hate crimes as a tool being used to hammer the agendas of special interests."* That is a legitimate question, but there are reasons why that story is not as compelling as the story of Matthew Shepard. Considering the business he is in, Bill O'Reilly should know that.

I vividly remember the news coverage of the brutal murder of Jesse Dirkhising, and it is true that Jesse's murder did not receive the same national attention as the murder of Matthew Shepard. It could easily be argued that both murders were equally brutal. Both murders involved heterosexual and homosexual victims *and* murderers. The news media often act in ways that defy the fairness and objectivity that once governed the decisions about which news stories to cover and how to cover those stories.

Groups that are perceived as being traditionally victimized by society fit perfectly with the preconceived biases of the general public. This reality is an integral part of the news media.

The original role of the news media was to expose the wrongdoing of powerful government on behalf of less powerful individual citizens. This gives the news media a David vs. Goliath role in society.

The next time you read or see news coverage of a train hitting a car, notice how the visual and verbal perspective seems to lead towards protection of the smaller and less powerful car, which was crushed by a big, powerful locomotive. But trains don't hit cars by veering off the tracks. Trains hit cars because of mistakes by motorists. Certainly there are exceptions, but the overwhelming number of car/train accidents result from negligence on the part of the driver of the car-not the engineer of the train.

Here's a vivid example of how the news media take advantage of preconceived images of certain groups. If Rodney King had been a white guy who was beaten by four black Los Angeles police officers, the national attention given the story would have been minimal. America will forever deal with the scars of slavery.

Victims from any group that has been traditionally discriminated against will always receive more media attention and perhaps more sympathy because the crime opens old and painful wounds. This is why white-on-black crimes will always attract more media attention than black-on-white, black-on-black, or white-on-white crimes. It doesn't have to be fair to be reality.

Because of the historic prejudice towards homosexuals, a crime committed by a **heterosexual** against a **homosexual** will always be enhanced by mainstream America's preconceived feelings about homosexuals.

Is every crime a *hate* crime?

The Random House Dictionary:

crime (krim), n. an action or an instance of negligence that is deemed injurious to the public welfare or morals. serious wrongdoing; sin.

All crimes are *not* hate crimes. It is easy to argue that any crime is an action motivated by some kind of hate or disregard for the rights of others, but the term "hate crime" accurately defines a specific type of crime.

If an armed man fatally shot a store clerk while robbing a store, it can be assumed that the armed man was not acting out of hate for the store clerk. His motivation was stealing money and the store clerk was an obstacle in achieving his goal. If a drunk driver kills a person while driving home drunk, the death resulted not from hate, but from reckless behavior. Two men get into a fistfight because one of the men was looking at the other man's girlfriend. The boyfriend started the fight, not out of hate for the other man, but to defend his girlfriend. All crimes are *not* hate crimes.

The term **hate crime** defines those crimes that *are* motivated by hatred of an entire group of people or an individual belonging to that group. Individuals become the victims of hatred directed towards a particular group. The most obvious hate crimes are the crimes inspired by hate for two groups—African Americans and homosexuals.

Our nation has a history of crimes committed against African Americans based solely on their skin color. The Civil Rights Act of 1964 established that all men (and women) are created equal. The act was a major step towards bringing an end to discrimination of blacks. And forty years later, hate crimes against African Americans continue. The crimes motivated by hatred of African Americans and homosexuals are distinctively different from other crimes. But there are parallels between the motivations of hate for homosexuals and the hate for African Americans, which are, in some places, still alive.

All of us are not civilized!

A painful reminder of the continuing presence of hate crimes can be found in the story of forty-nine-year-old James Byrd. Mr. Byrd was killed on June 7, 1998, after three white males dragged him behind a pickup truck near Jasper, Texas. In fairness to the entire state of Texas, Jasper is in east Texas, which is close to the state line with Louisiana. East Texas has more in common with Louisiana, Mississippi, Alabama, and Georgia than with the rest of Texas. In other words, racism is still celebrated.

On the night of June 7, 1998, John William King, Shawn Allen Berry, and Lawrence Russell Brewer were out joyriding in a pickup truck. At one point, they used a logging chain in the truck to pull down a mailbox in front of a Jasper house. Later that evening, the three white males came upon James Byrd, who was drunk and walking home from a party. Berry offered him a ride—a ride he should never have accepted.

James Byrd and the three white males ended up on a logging road about six miles east of Jasper. This is where they stopped and, in court testimony, Brewer quoted Mr. Byrd as saying, *"Let me smoke with you white boys."* Next, King and Mr. Byrd were on the ground, fighting. Brewer testified that he kicked Mr. Byrd in the ribs when the fight began and sprayed Byrd's face with black paint.

Berry then approached Byrd and it is believed that is when Berry slashed James Byrd's throat.

James Byrd was chained by his ankles to the pickup truck and dragged for three to three and a half miles down a road. His body was found in pieces along the road. An autopsy showed that Mr. Byrd was alive when the three white males began dragging him behind the truck. The injuries also revealed that Mr. Bryd struggled to hold his head up off the road while he was being dragged. His body, or what was left of it, was abandoned in front of a predominantly black church.

Prosecutors in the case argued that James Byrd was murdered to gain attention for a racist group, which Brewer and King were starting. Police found twenty-two pages of documents that would have established the bylaws of a racist group to be called the "Confederate Knights of America Texas Rebel Soldiers."

One of the white men, Lawrence Russell Brewer, was a thirty-two-year-old ex-con. On the Web page of the Texas NAACP, there is this account of part of Brewer's testimony: Brewer *"broke into choking sobs and turned his back on the courtroom as defense attorney Layne Walker showed him autopsy pictures of James Bryd's mutilated body.* In the courtroom, Brewer said, *'I don't want to look at them pictures. I don't want to look at them.'"*

John William King: <u>convicted</u> of capital murder and sentenced to **death**.

Shawn Allen Berry: <u>convicted</u> of capital murder and sentenced to **death**.

Lawrence Russell Brewer: <u>convicted</u> of murder and sentenced to **life**.

Three white males killed a black man by dragging him behind a truck just because of the hatred they had for blacks. This hate crime occurred in 1998. Didn't word of the Civil Rights Act of 1964 reach east Texas?

Matthew Shepard and James Byrd were killed because of hate. Yet many continue to argue that crimes motivated by hate do no deserve special penalties.

Hate crime legislation

Currently, there is an attempt to revise the Hate Crimes Prevention Act to include crimes committed out of hate based on sexual orientation, gender, or disability. The bill, known as the Local Law Enforcement Act, would change the existing legislation by describing a "hate crime" as a violent act causing death or bodily injury because of the actual or perceived race, color, religion, national origin, sexual orientation, gender, or disability. This legislation is not designed to give homosexuals special rights, but it does recognize the need for added protection. The motivation behind the legislation is the need to balance the protection for individuals of groups that are brutally victimized simply for belonging to certain groups that have historically been discriminated against.

FBI hate crime statistics for 2001, the most recent available, show a total of 9,730 hate crimes committed. Race was the reason for 4,367 hate crimes; ethnicity/national origin accounted for 2,098. Religion was the motivation that led to 1,828 hate crimes. And 1,393 hate crimes were motivated out of hate for an individual's sexual orientation. These numbers are small in comparison to overall crime statistics, but considering the percentage of gays and lesbians in context of the overall population in America, the number of hate crimes committed against homosexuals is significant enough to address.

Hate crimes against people based on their sexual orientation have increased since 1992. In that year, 767 hate crimes were based on sexual orientation. In 1995, homosexuals were the targets of 1,019 hate crimes. By 1998, 1,260 homosexuals had been attacked simply because of the way they engage in private sex acts. In 2001, hate crimes against homosexuals had risen to 1,393. And there is every reason to believe that a much greater number of hate crimes go unreported.

As the acceptance of homosexuality continues to reach deeper into the mainstream population, there may be a growing backlash. A *USA Today*/CNN/Gallup Poll was conducted in May and again in June of 2003 on the issue of whether homosexual sex should be legal. In May 2003, 59 percent said it should be legal. In July, just a few months later, 50 percent of the respondents agreed that homosexual sex should be legal. A CBS/*New York Times* poll showed in July of 2003, that 54 percent of Americans believed gay sex should be legal.

Through the 1990s, over 60 percent of those polled said they opposed same-sex marriages. Before 2003, four Gallup Polls asked, would you *"favor or oppose a law that would allow homosexual couples to legally form a civil union, giving them some of the legal rights of married couples?"* The percentage of those supporting legal civil unions for gay couples ranged from 44 percent to 46 percent in three of the four polls. Opposition ranged from 51 percent to 53 percent in three of the four polls.

In May of 2003, the Gallup Poll showed that 49 percent of the respondents favored civil unions for gays and 49 percent opposed. By July of 2003, 57 percent *opposed* civil unions for gays and 40 percent favored legal civil unions. From May 2003 to June 2003, support for civil unions for homosexuals dropped 9 percent, while opposition increased 8 percent. These figures represent a backlash from the heterosexual community, which is now facing the real possibility of gay marriage becoming legal.

Should homosexual relations between consenting adults be legal? That has been a Gallup Poll question for years. In 1977, 43 percent supported sodomy laws while 43 percent opposed them. By 1982, 45 percent favored legalizing sodomy and 39 percent opposed it. I wonder how many of the heterosexuals responding to these polls realized that heterosexual oral and anal sex is sodomy. If you're opposed to sodomy for gays, then you should oppose straight married couples engaging in sodomy.

The Pew Research Center for the People and the Press conducted a national poll, which asked the question, *"Should teachers who are known to be homosexuals be fired?"* The 1987 results showed 51 percent favored firing a gay teacher, and in 1997, the number dropped to 33 percent.

These polls do show some progress in the battle for equal rights for gays and lesbians, but we have a long way to go. Undoubtedly, the "mother of all battles" in the war over equal rights for gays and lesbians will come when all the troops line up to fight the battle over legislation that would define a marriage in America as a union between a man and a woman. The year 2004 will be remembered as the year the civil rights battle over gay marriage began.

In October of 2003, A *USA Today*/CNN/Gallup Poll showed 77 percent of eighteen- to twenty-four-year-olds had no opposition to legal marriages for gay and lesbian couples. In the age group of thirty- to forty-nine-year-olds, support was 65 percent and still a majority of 60 percent of those fifty to sixty-four responded that they were not opposed to homosexual marriages. But that would soon change.

United we stand—divided we fall-into groups

One of the major changes in America over the past two decades has been the separation of individuals by groups. From the beginning, America has been a collection of individuals with a common bond. Today, however, America has become a nation of groups made up of individuals bound together by different common denominators.

Any individual can claim membership in several different groups, but there will be a primary alliance with one particular group. Claiming membership in a group may change to conveniently fit an issue that is drawing national attention. *"There is power in victimization,"* wrote professor and author Shelby Steele.

I don't deny that many individuals seek membership in certain groups for the vicarious attention derived from the controversy surrounding that particular group. For example, a heterosexual, white, Republican male becomes primarily a heterosexual in a debate over gay rights. The same individual might feel more aligned with whites in a conflict over race. He or she would, of course, proudly own membership in the Republican Party when the debate turns to politics.

Prior to the political conventions in the summer of 2004, America had reached a point of unprecedented divide between Republicans and Democrats. The great division continued after Bush won the election. Membership in either political party seemed to be more important than a unified America.

During the presidential campaign of 2004, being a Republican or a Democrat seemed more important than being an American. We should always be Americans first and Democrats or Republicans second. But the campaign of 2004 will be remembered as the campaign that caused citizens to announce allegiance to their party first and their country second.

The number of groups opposing each other has grown to a level that demonstrates how determined Americans are to seek identity through a group, rather than their innate individuality.

Here is a list of a few groups that have developed hate for each other over the past twenty:

Republicans vs. Democrats
heterosexuals vs. homosexuals
Pro-Iraqi War vs. Anti-Iraqi War
whites vs. blacks
white vs. Hispanics
smokers vs. non-smokers
SUV drivers vs. all other motorists
urbanites vs. suburbanites
metrosexuals vs. macho straight men
snowboarders vs. skiers
rockers vs. rappers
men vs. women
war veterans vs. non-military citizens
cat lovers vs. dog lovers
Christians vs. Jews
Christians & Jews vs. Muslims
home owners vs. homeless
rich vs. poor

Imagine the animosity that might exist between **a straight white Christian Republican, who smokes, lives in the suburbs, drives an SUV, hates snowboarders, listens to rock music and owns a dog…and a gay black Democrat who supports anti-smoking legislation, lives in the city, uses public transportation, enjoys snowboarding, owns a cat, protests all wars, and is a vegetarian with limited discretionary income!**

Understanding the phenomenon of belonging to a group is important to fully understanding the battle over gay rights.

A growing number of Americans are prone to define their identity by the group or groups to which they belong. The ease with which new groups are forming and attracting instant members is a testament to the widening chasm that divides America.

The pace of our world set by rapidly advancing technology has reached an overwhelming point. New technology is both positive and negative. The positive side is more obvious, while the negative power of technology has a less revealing impact on society.

The ability to use computers to pay bills, conduct banking transactions, buy virtually any product, send mail instantly around the world, and find virtually any bit of information may be viewed as a welcomed convenience. But it is the speed of technology's advancement into the world of warm-blooded humans that inspires resistance to change. It's instinctive to fear the unknown of a rapidly approaching future.

Through the course of an evolving society, America has lost a sense of community. Yet, in the busy, entertainment-driven, high-tech world that surrounds us, we are craving that lost sense of community.

One of the primary reasons Starbucks continues to be successful is because it provides the opportunity to experience a sense of community. Starbucks' latte may be exceptional, but exceptional latte can be found in many different places. It is the atmosphere Starbucks offers that makes it unique and popular. A group of complete strangers sharing a common locale can satisfy a desire for community. As loose as it may be, strangers can share a common bond.

After spending hours writing in my loft apartment in downtown Denver, I decided to get out, but I wanted to continue writing. So there I was sitting in a Starbucks on the 16th Mall in downtown Denver. As I continued to write this book with my laptop, I was experiencing a sense of community from the strangers sitting around me.

The need for community is not primarily based on communicating with others. We innately crave the need to be seen by others as confirmation that we exist as human beings. Having dinner alone in a crowded restaurant is different from eating the same meal at home alone. Walking down a street alone with no other person in sight is different from walking down a crowded street passing unknown faces.

Continuing my writing at Starbucks, I would occasionally glance up and peer out of the window at the many pedestrians walking along the crowded mall. I focused on a male teen dressed in black Goth attire with black lipstick and numerous visible piercings. He was standing on the sidewalk with the obvious goal of being noticed, even if in a negative way. He wanted to be recognized by others for who he was, even by those who may have thought he looked ridiculous. This Goth teenager did not dress up and just sit at home. His goal was to be noticed by others as he made an obvious anti-establishment statement with his appearance in public.

We all want to be acknowledged, even by total strangers. The various and annoying rings and loud talking on cell phones in public are irritating. If you are in a line, walking close to someone, or sitting next to a table where someone is talking on a cell phone, you get the feeling that the person using the phone is not recognizing your existence. The stranger on the phone is focusing their attention on the person on the other end. We don't necessarily have a desire to talk to any of these people, but the cell phone takes away the feeling of being acknowledged by others. We are afraid of being anonymous.

The Internet provides another sense of community, especially for younger generations. This new ability to communicate with others without personal contact provides a sense of being part of a community while maintaining isolation. Chat rooms and message boards bring individuals together as a community. Television was the first medium that began to isolate us as individuals. Now, the computer has created more opportunity for isolation, while at the same time bringing people together.

I realized exactly what television had done to us as a society during one of the powerful thunderstorms so typical in New Orleans in the summer. Lightning had knocked out the electricity. Neighbors walked out of their homes and joined on the sidewalk to talk about what happened and when the electricity might be restored.

It was amazing to witness people who did not even known each other's names brought together as a "group" that shared the common bond of having lost power. Had the electricity not gone out, those neighbors would have remained in their homes watching television, cooking, or whatever. The formation of that spontaneous neighborhood group was proof that a mass communication system had robbed individuals of their *need* to talk to one another… unless the electricity went out!

Talk radio has become the second most popular radio format in the nation. The country music format is number one, but the prominence of talk radio has skyrocketed since the '80s. Every day people tune into talk radio, not just to be enlightened about the top political and social issues of the day, but also to feel part of a community. Tuning into talk radio makes a lone motorist stuck in traffic feel as if he or she is connected with others listening to the same talk show.

It is only about 10 percent of any talk radio audience that actually calls in to participate. But those who never call into a show vicariously become part of the community of listeners through the callers who reflect a similar point-of-view or an opposite point-of-view. It is a mental presence rather than physical presence that creates the community through radio. But it is still a community.

As mentioned earlier, the homosexual community is tightly bound by an understanding of their sexual preference, which is contrary to mainstream America. And the anti-gay community is bound by their condemnation of the homosexual lifestyle through common religious beliefs, which also creates a very strong bond.

Innate sexual preference and the adherence to Biblical scripture are two powerful forces that will cause these two groups to repel each other forever. This is not to suggest that one side will not be victorious over the other, but there will *never* be a mutual agreement on the issue of gay rights.

[I'm still writing at Starbucks. A man just sat down next me and let out a huge sigh, followed by an almost inaudible "fuck," in what was an obvious attempt to make others take note of his presence. The more I remained focused on my writing, the more this man tried to get me to make eye contact with him as a way of acknowledging his existence. The world we have created isolates us and yet we seek a sense of community and recognition that we exist in that world.]

PART III

Chapter 6

Hollywood *Loves* Homosexuals!

Since gays and lesbians have *always* been part of our society, why then shouldn't the homosexual lifestyle be reflected in the media? There has been an increase in the number of homosexual characters on television. The Religious Right is worried that the presence of more gay and lesbian characters on television will lead to further acceptance of homosexuality. And further acceptance of homosexuality is what the Religious Right so greatly fears.

Any group's battle for equality pits one side against another side. It is the compelling conflict between the two groups that attracts mainstream media attention.

Through the extensive media coverage of the beginning of the battle over gay marriage in early 2004, gays and lesbians have become more compelling as an entertainment commodity. Consistent attention from the news media builds the foundation for the general public's growing interest in homosexuals, whether positive or negative.

This familiarity is essential before homosexual characters could become part of mainstream entertainment. Comedy and drama are based on actual life. Ask Shakespeare, Oliver Stone, or Mel Gibson. The more often visuals of the members of a minority group are seen by a mass audience, the more likely it is that the entertainment industry will instinctively take advantage of the increased familiarity of the group. The entertainment industry is always anxious to discover a new group around which it can build new entertainment.

The prime time TV shows from the past were simplistic, phony, and unrealistic. *The Dick Van Dyke Show, Father Knows Best, Happy Days,* and many others would not be popular prime time shows today. The programs that are now classics would not work in the context of today's society. Storylines about raising families, dating, relationships, school and work do transcend generations, but the characters, the settings and the content of entertainment today must reflect a culture that is constantly shaped by the world around it.

Norman Lear sent television in a bold new direction in the '70s. Lear's vision was so controversial that it would be fair to consider him the Howard Stern of television. With TV shows like *All in the Family* and *Maude,* America suddenly found controversial issues from the real world coming into their living rooms. Sex, drugs, abortion, rape, the anti-war protesting from the Vietnam era, and even homosexuality were all issues that became part of Norman Lear's innovative approach to television.

Watching a rerun of *All in the Family* is almost like watching a satire of a current sitcom, but the edginess of the show would never be tolerated in today's more politically correct world. The use of words to satirically degrade minorities and our two political parties would be widely condemned. Ironically, *All in the Family* is currently airing in reruns on the TV Land network.

I find it interesting that TV shows in reruns contain content that would not be allowed in current programs. Archie Bunker, the primary character in *All in the Family* used the word "fag" to refer to gay males. Andy Griffith, Lucille Ball, and Dick Van Dyke all smoked cigarettes on camera. And young people are watching those reruns on TV Land! Why is there no concern for the impact of smoking in TV shows from our past? Imagine if Will and Grace or characters in *Everyone Loves Raymond* smoked cigarettes. But it would be different. The content that would be considered too controversial today is softened by the realization that those programs reflect past attitudes and not present day.

In television shows from the '50s and '60s, like *Leave it to Beaver,* the mother, June Cleaver wore a dress with pearls every day, all day. The father, Ward Cleaver, would come home from work and sit at the dinner table with the family, still wearing his coat and tie. Ward would even relax on the sofa wearing his coat and tie as he read the newspaper. That wasn't anything I saw in my home, growing up! Looking back those TV shows were not relatable.

I lived in the exact kind of neighborhood the Cleavers lived in and my parents were never dressed up at home. Was my dear mother a slob because she wore shorts, a blouse and sandals when she cleaned the house or went to the store? June Cleaver, Donna Reed, and Margaret Anderson were TV mothers who did not reflect the reality of the years those shows were popular.

It is true that TV shows from the '50s and '60s did not represent real world reality, but that does not contradict the fact that those shows *were* reflective of American culture at the time. The content audiences wanted in the past is quite different from the content audience demand today. Realistic content about real life is critical to attracting the more cynical audiences of today.

So how does this relate to the fight for gay rights in America? In order to defuse the criticism that Hollywood has an agenda of *promoting* gay rights, it is imperative to understand some of the forces that govern the entertainment and news media.

Television shows are products to be consumed by consumers. In their book, *Under the Radar: Talking to Today's Cynical Consumers*, authors Jonathan Bond and Richard Kirshenbaum address the difficulty of attracting today's consumers. Consumers have developed "radar" that alerts them to tune out radio and TV commercials. In order to reach consumers, it has become necessary to get the message of a commercial "under the radar" that alerts these consumers to ignore the message.

Honesty and authenticity are key elements. In writing about their client, Snapple, Bond and Kirshenbaum explain why they used "Wendy," an overweight, very average-looking spokesperson for the product: *"Any company willing to show you its true self, warts and all, is one you can trust, we thought."*

Entertainment, like advertising, faces the challenge of attracting the attention of an audience that has become over stimulated with hundreds and hundreds of messages and bits of information every minute of every day.

Though television shows are exaggerated to create compelling entertainment, the content of the shows and characters must be more realistic than in the past. A program like *Father Knows Best*, along with that genre of family oriented sitcoms, would be too unrealistic to succeed in attracting an audience today.

One of the most popular programs through the conservative '80s was *The Cosby Show*. The Huxtable family was respectful, and reflected the moral attitude in the 80s. I have tried watching reruns of *The Cosby Show*, but find the content and the characters impossible to relate to today.

The first TV sitcom to feature a modern, realistic relationship between husband, wife, and children was *Roseanne.* On the show, the parents loved their kids, but they were honest about how kids can be very aggravating. For that reason, reruns of *Roseanne* are easier to relate to than reruns of *The Cosby Show.*

Reality isn't *real* on TV

The new genre of TV *reality shows*, from *Survivor* to *The Bachelor* has been successful because the shows are real. Well, reality TV shows are only as real as the medium of television will allow them to be.

Every reality-based TV show must be produced for the medium of television. Reality shows don't have actors or actual scripts, but each show does have a producer who must understand what makes shows successful on television. The content of these shows is guided by producers who know how to attract and hold the attention of an audience by developing characters and a storyline out of a show with no script. Reality television is only *real* in the context of the programming that has set the standards for successful television.

Here's a classic example of how reality shows are guided by producers. In 2003, Clay and Reuben reached the finals on *American Idol*. There should have been little doubt as to who would be the winner. Clay had talent and possessed star quality, which is rare. He was lean with a very hip hairstyle, similar to what one might see in MTV videos.

Reuben was very talented, but completely lacked star quality. He was also grossly overweight. From the description of Reuben and Clay, which one do you think won the competition? Oh, one more important factor. Clay was white and Reuben was black.

I do not believe that the producers of that edition of *American Idol* would have allowed the lean white guy to beat the over weight black guy. I certainly do not intend for that to sound racist, but that is the reality of *reality* television. Past wounds continue to create great sensitivity to anything that might be perceived as racist. If Clay had beaten Reuben, the outcome would have reinforced white privilege and the advantage of being more visually attractive.

I'm convinced the producers of the show made sure the judges knew which outcome would be more desirable. In fact, Reuben may have been carried to the end to set up the dramatic contrast for the finale. Reuben won. That's not to suggest that whites hold a singing superiority to blacks, but in the situation, the best talent didn't win because he was white. That should never happen, but it does happen because the goal of television as a medium is to attract the largest possible audience.

What happened in the weeks and months after the show confirms that my observations about that edition of *American Idol* are accurate. Clay, the one who finished second to Reuben, released a CD shortly after the show ended and it shot to number one on the charts. Reuben did not experience that kind of success until about a year later.

TV shows like *Survivor, The Apprentice,* and *The Bachelor,* have producers that take advantage of every opportunity to edit each edition as to create an image for each of the contestants. The images created are those the producers believe are the most compelling to a viewing audience. Even though reality-based TV shows have no specific script, predetermined themes can be easily created through editing. *Real* reality television would be so boring, few would watch.

Queer Eye for the Straight Guy, which airs on the Bravo Cable Network, is as close to a *real* reality TV show as you'll find on television. The show features five homosexual males taking on the challenge of making a *straight* male more appealing to the straight woman in his life. The five gay men, known as the Fab 5, each have an area of expertise. There is a fashion expert, a food and wine expert, a culture consultant, an interior design professional, and a personal grooming expert.

At the beginning of each show, the Fab 5 arrive at a straight guy's apartment or house in SWAT-team style! They jump out of their shiny black SUV and rush to the door. Once inside, each guy attacks his area of expertise. The fashion expert goes to the straight guy's closet and begins making fun of all of the clothes. The culture expert starts going through the CD collection and checks out the guy's books and magazines. The food and wine expert heads into what is always a very messy and disgusting kitchen, usually with dishes covered with old crusty food stacked in the sink. And the grooming expert goes to the straight guy's repulsive bathroom and beings going through the grooming products.

Queer Eye for the Straight Guy was successful instantly. But why? First of all, the show was unique and innovative. More importantly, it gave straight America a voyeuristic view into the differences between the way heterosexuals and homosexuals view themselves and the world around them. There are the obvious sexual differences, but *Queer Eye* allowed the gay guys to completely be themselves with gestures, phrases, speech patterns, and content that fit America's stereotypical image of homosexual males. They were all natural but that doesn't mean they all appeared obviously gay.

The concept of the show conjures up the reality that gay men are more artistic and fashion-conscious than straight men. Gay men have the instincts to turn straight men into more attractive prospects for straight women. Ironic, isn't it?

There has been so much spiteful debating between the gay community and heterosexuals that *Queer Eye* brought the two worlds together through the process of gay men helping straight men. There is an unmentioned undertone in the show that goes mostly unnoticed. The Fab 5 demonstrate that most straight guys actually *need* gay guys to help them become more attractive to straight women.

There are certainly many straight guys, who defiantly argue that they do not need the help of gay men, but those guys are either in denial or reluctant to admit the obvious. **Metrosexuals** are the only males who may not be in desperate need of help from homosexuals. [Metrosexuals are defined in Chapter 9.]

The brilliance of *Queer Eye for the Straight Guy* stems from the sincere—if not at times sarcastic—desire to help transform straight men with bad hair, filthy apartments cluttered with junk, outdated clothes, and kitchens where one can finds the equivalent of the biological and chemical weapons the U.S. was searching for in Iraq.

Queer Eye is fast-paced, well directed, and compelling. At the end of each show, the Fab 5 give final instructions to the straight guy, who has morphed into a new person. At this point, the Fab 5 dash off in their black SUV and head to a posh apartment where they all sit on a half circle sofa in front of a wide, flat-screen television monitor on the wall. This is where they watch the guy they just made over either do, or *not do*, all the things he was taught. It's similar to a coach who does all he can to prepare his team for a game and hopes the team will do it right on game day.

As the Fab 5 watch the action with drinks in hand, there is screaming at the TV screen with the excitement of die-hard football fans watching their team play. The Fab 5 sit around discussing how successful they were in turning a sloppy straight guy into a very stylish guy who is suddenly more attractive to a straight woman.

Queer Eye for the Straight Guy is the first show to establish a meaningful on-camera relationship between straight guys and gay guys. The visual image of that bonding is a good message in the growing debate over gay equality.

Queer Eye was so successful that NBC, the company that owns the Bravo channel, decided to run several of the hour-long episodes on NBC during prime time. If there had not been mainstream heterosexual acceptance and curiosity about a meeting of the gay and straight worlds, *Queer Eye for the Straight Guy* would not have become so successful.

So the question to be answered is *why* was *Queer Eye for the Straight Guy* successful at a time when there has been an increasing debate over homosexual rights? Never have the two worlds engaged in such harsh debate. Consider how significant it is for straight guys to accept lifestyle tips from homosexual men. Even more interesting is the fact that straight guys can't really offer any advice on how to help gay guys be more attractive to gay guys!

In early December 2003, the Web site, *ZAP2IT.com* quoted a study conducted by a New York-based public relations firm that could have given credence to the argument that media directly effect the behavior of the audience. The public relations study indicated that men were *five* times more likely than women to go shopping at a mall on the Wednesday after *Queer Eye* aired in its original time slot on Tuesday evenings. The study also showed that after men watched the show, nearly *half* said they would ask a guy friend to go shopping with them! What?! Heterosexual men asking male friends to go shopping with them?

In shopping malls in Boston, New York, Chicago, Los Angeles, San Francisco, Washington, and suburban Philadelphia, people were asked what celebrity they trusted most in the endorsement of products. The answer? Carson, the most flamboyant of the Fab 5 on *Queer Eye for the Straight Guy*, was the top selection at 15 percent. California's governor, Arnold Schwarzenegger, was second with 13 percent. L.A. Lakers' superstar Kobe Bryant, who at the time was accused of sexual assault, was third. Ashton Kutcher was fourth, and Ben Affleck and Paris Hilton tied for fifth. The general shopping public at malls across America selected a homosexual male as the celebrity who had the *most* credibility with endorsing products! That's progress the Religious Right would never want to acknowledge.

Does the direct response from an audience illustrate that entertainment *does* directly affect the behavior of the audience? If you interpret the information about men, presumably straight men, changing their behavior because of what they have viewed on television on the surface, the evidence towards effecting behavior appears compelling.

However, it is more reasonable to believe that the content on *Queer Eye* simply brought out suppressed ideas within each individual straight male. Many straight men would not have followed the suggestions on *Queer Eye*.

Entertainment does inspire ideas, but entertainment does not have the power to convince individual audience members to act in a way that is not congruent with their innermost feelings. If a survey revealed that men were five times more likely to go shopping at a mall after watching *Queer Eye for the Straight Guy*, that means the TV show encouraged those men to act on an idea that fit their innate tendencies. It is not logical to believe that a fundamentalist Christian male who condemns homosexuality on religious grounds would change his style after watching *Queer Eye.* It is, however, reasonable to believe that a straight male who goes out to nightclubs to meet women and tries to be stylish would act upon suggestions that might help him become more attractive to the opposite sex. With those men, the desire to become more fashionable and more attractive to women was a predisposed condition.

Contrary to popular *right-wing* belief....

Queer Eye for the Straight Guy, Will & Grace, and any other TV shows or movies that feature gay characters are not vehicles created to advance the agenda of liberals in Hollywood. Gay-oriented programs and movies reflect the real world we live in, which is something many conservatives are reluctant to acknowledge.

Heterosexual America made TV programs and movies with dominate gay characters successful. If *every* homosexual in America watched a certain program there would not be enough viewers to justify it remaining on mainstream television. That is reality, not criticism. It takes heterosexuals to make a TV show a ratings success.

Will & Grace has consistently been one of the top-rated television shows in America, which means that a mass **heterosexual** audience has chosen it as a source of entertainment. No one is forced to watch the show. The sitcom is based on a successful gay attorney, Will, and his best friend, Grace, a straight female who works in the design industry. Grace has a job most people would expect the gay character to have and Will is a lawyer. Will and Grace are the primary characters, but it is clearly the characters of Jack, a flamboyant gay male, and Karen, a straight nymphomaniac lush who works with Grace that create a fertile setting for comedy.

Will & Grace is one of the most popular sitcoms on television because the characters are well defined and the situations between straight women and gay guys are ripe for comedy. The special relationship between Will and Grace demonstrates the advantages of friendships between heterosexuals and homosexuals. [Chapter 10: my special relationship with a lesbian!]

Then why Did *Ellen* Fail?

The ABC sitcom, *Ellen* was not successful in the long run. The fact that the show's lead character was a lesbian was not the reason for the downfall of *Ellen.* There were other factors that contributed to the demise of the show.

The audience knew Ellen was a lesbian because the show was peppered with subtleties suggesting her sexual orientation. But Ellen was not out of the closet on the show. In an effort to create buzz, the producers and writers decided to have Ellen—played by Ellen Degeneres, who is a lesbian—"come out" on the show. The "coming out" episode did attract a great deal of attention; much of it was negative attention from the Christian right.

The problem with Ellen admitting she was a lesbian after the show had been on the air caused the audience to feel deceived since she was not openly gay in the earlier episodes. After all the attention from the "coming out" episode, *Ellen* died a quick death.

Sitcoms are exaggerated depictions of real life. Still, the characters must have credibility within the fictional setting. Successful sitcoms like, *All in the Family, Fresh Prince of Bel-Air,* or even *Happy Days,* were all built around characters that won the trust of the audience.

In 2004, Ellen Degeneres began a TV talk show on the Oxygen network that was an instant success with critics and immediately attracted an audience. In the setting of a talk show format, Ellen was real and her sexual orientation was public knowledge. There was no deception. Audiences today demand honesty and reality.

I experienced a real-life scenario similar to what brought *Ellen* to its end. While doing a radio talk show in New Orleans, one of the afternoon co-hosts, a guy named Gary Spears, was, in reality, gay. Everyone at the radio station knew it, but his radio audience had no idea.

As a **metrosexual**, I was an easy target for some of my competitors. There were a few talk show hosts that felt the need to portray me as being "gay." The general bias against homosexuals motivated these radio morons to try to degrade me by suggesting that I was gay. One talk show host even called me a pedophile on his show. That was slander, but I decided to remain above the fray and not retaliate.

Gary Spears' did the afternoon show on WEZB-FM in New Orleans with a guy named Steve Johnson, who was once a competitor of mine on another radio station in the city. Steve became the afternoon host on the radio station where I was hosting the midday show. Steve introduced his new partner, Gary, to the running joke that I was gay.

There were comments about my alleged sexual preference constantly being made by Steve and Gary. I found it laughable that Gary, a homosexual who hid his orientation on the air, would dare try to put me down by suggesting that *I* was gay! I ignored all the comments and never responded...until one day.

One morning at 10:00am I opened my show saying, *"Enough of this talk about me being gay."* And the rant continued for the entire show. Many listeners called to say they never thought I was gay because they had known some of the women I had been with, including two wives. In fact, two ex-girlfriends called the show that day to set the record straight with their admission of firsthand experience! I always considered it such an insult to the homosexual community, which is significant in New Orleans, that these radio buffoons thought that labeling me gay was a form of degradation. But my revenge was yet to be realized.

Steve had resigned over a contract dispute and Gary found himself doing the afternoon show alone. One day, Gary decided to be honest with the audience in an attempt to create buzz for his afternoon show, which was not doing well. Without notice, Gary Spears "outed" himself on the air in hopes his honest confession about being gay would endear him to his audience.

What Gary Spears discovered was an audience that immediately rejected him, not because he was gay, but because the audience felt deceived by the charade that he was straight. The next day, on the air, I received numerous calls from listeners who realized that while Spears had been trying to put me down by suggesting that I gay.... he was gay!

My revenge was realized when my credibility skyrocketed after Gary admitted that he was gay. His loss was my gain. The audience realized that during the many verbal putdowns of me, I could have "outed" Gary on the air, but I never did. Gary's ratings collapsed and he was fired. Revenge has no after taste!

Blame it all on *straight* audiences!

Here's one of many examples. The smash hit movie, *The Birdcage* starred Robin Williams as a divorced father who was gay and living with his partner, played by Nathan Lane. Gene Hackman played a very conservative politician in Washington, whose daughter, played by a young Calista Flockhart, was engaged to the son of Robin Williams. The daughter's conservative family had no reason to believe that her fiancé's father was gay.

There was comic anxiety when it was time for the conservative politician and his wife to meet the parents of their daughter's fiancé. A conservative politician meeting Robin Williams' character and Nathan Lane's character, who was in drag pretending to be Williams' wife, set the stage for a fresh perspective on the age-old cinematic scenario of two sets of parents of an engaged couple meeting for the first time. It wasn't that the majority of the audience had actually experienced the actual moments depicted in the movie, but the audience could relate to how they *might* deal with a similar situation.

For several consecutive weeks, *The Birdcage* was the number one movie in America. Factually, there are not enough homosexuals in America to make a movie number one at the box office. Again, fact-not criticism. The point to be made is that it was *straight* America that flocked to see the movie in massive numbers.

Were *straight* Americans forced to go see *The Birdcage*? Did the liberals of Hollywood make the movie in an attempt to force homosexuality as normal in America? You know the answer to those questions, but the Religious Right doesn't want to accept the reality that such a large number of heterosexuals supported a movie with a gay theme.

In spite of the public opinion polls, which showed that somewhere between 55 percent and 60 percent of Americans opposed gay marriage, there is an innate, yet rarely admitted, heterosexual curiosity about the gay lifestyle. Heterosexuals are curious about homosexuals because of the fundamental differences in the primal instinct of sex. Human nature leads us to have greater interest in those who are different. As mentioned earlier, the TV reality show, *Queer Eye for the Straight Guy*, allowed heterosexuals to watch gay males reveal aspects of their homosexuality through the process of explaining what they thought was wrong with straight guys.

Queer Eye for the Straight Guy showed us that gay guys can help straight guys...but can straight guys help gay guys?

I settled a domestic quarrel between Richard Simmons and his boyfriend one night in Los Angeles. My friendship with Richard Simmons began in New Orleans when I did some announcing for one of Richard's TV shows in the mid-'80s. He had also been on my radio show several times. So, while in L.A. for business, I called Richard and he invited me to dinner. After downing sushi at a restaurant, Richard was driving his white Mercedes down Sunset Boulevard with his boyfriend in the front seat and me in the back seat. At one point, Richard looked at me in the rearview mirror and asked me if I had ever had sex with a man. I answered honestly, *"No."* Then Richard made the comment that if I ever *did* have sex with a man, I would never go back to women. To which I replied, *"Don't be so sure!"*

After dinner that night in Los Angeles, we all went back to Richard's beautiful home in the hills off Sunset Boulevard. We were all sitting around the kitchen table when the conversation erupted into a domestic quarrel between Richard and his boyfriend. Have you ever been in the presence of a couple that got into a heated argument? That's the way I felt!

I don't remember everything, but Richard's boyfriend said he was fed up with Richard getting all the attention wherever they went. Then he made a comment about Richard finding a new "boy toy" as soon as they had broken up recently. I do remember pointing out the merits of each side of the argument and then reaching a mutual agreement. The rest of the evening was spent talking and watching television. I never really knew why Richard Simmons asked me if I have ever had sex with a man.

Does television have the power to *hurt* gay America?

Whenever debating the idea that entertainment causes negative behavior in society on talk radio, I consistently heard the argument that *if television did not have the ability to change behavior, then why do so many companies spend millions and millions of dollars on their commercials?* This might appear to be a difficult point to rebut if you believe that TV and entertainment, in general, are responsible for negative behavior; however it actually solidifies my argument that entertainment, and TV commercials, *do not* possess the power to make individuals do something they really don't want to do.

Be honest with yourself. Can you think of even *one* TV commercial that made you do something you really didn't want to do?

If a person is overweight and is not ready to commit to losing weight, a TV commercial for a fitness club will not cause that person to join the club and lose weight. But the overweight individual who really wants to do something about their weight but hasn't done anything about it yet, might respond to a fitness club commercial.

If a twenty-five-year-old male is not a beer drinker, a Coors Light commercial, no matter how entertaining and convincing, will not turn a non-beer-drinking guy into a beer drinker. If a person has no desire to purchase a new car, the most compelling car advertisement will not convince that person to go out and buy a new car. However, if a person is thinking about buying a new car, or at least realizes he or she needs a new car, then a TV commercial for a particular dealership might just convince that person to buy a car from the dealership that paid for the commercial.

By the way, have you thought of a TV commercial that influenced you to do something you really didn't want to do?

I didn't think so!

It is important to understand the forces that drive entertainment and advertising in order to understand how the mass media affects the image of gay and lesbian population. The success of gay TV shows and gay characters, especially during prime time hours when younger viewers are most available, has attracted increased criticism of "liberal" Hollywood's alleged gay agenda.

Let's go back at the principles that govern entertainment and advertising. **Entertainment and advertising cannot drive an individual to act in a way that is not congruent with predisposed innate behavior.**

The lack of a true understanding of the relationship between mass media and society is a frightening reality in America. An overwhelming number of consumers of mass media possess a dangerous misunderstanding of the role mass media plays in our culture. The idea that television programming has the ability to dictate negative behavior in the real world is based on a naïve and superficial understanding of mass media.

When behavior in the real world appears to mirror behavior in mass media, the immediate assumption is that mass media has set new standards and dictates actions considered inappropriate in the real world. There is a never-ending debate concerning communication theory. Does entertainment and advertising *reflect* the collective audience or *dictate* the behavior of the audience?

It could be argued that both are true. However, my constant studying of the question has led me to the conclusion that there is much more evidence indicating that entertainment and advertising *reflect*, rather than *dictate* the behavior of an audience. If an individual audience member reacts to an idea presented in entertainment or in advertising, the individual did not act solely on the idea without an innate proclivity towards the idea.

The growing number of homosexual characters on prime time television will **not** cause young audience members to become gay anymore than violence in prime time viewing hours will inspire young audience members to become violent. Contrary to what many might believe, there is absolutely **no** conclusive evidence to support the theory that gays on television will cause more people to become gay or that violence in entertainment encourages real-world violence. The concern that gay and lesbian acceptance in entertainment will lead us to the moral downfall of American society is the rhetoric of the Religious Right's agenda of imposing their religious beliefs on others.

The entertainment industry has not done a very good job of defending itself and convincing mainstream America that there is not a direct connection between entertainment and inappropriate real-world behavior. I'm not suggesting that homosexual behavior is inappropriate, but that is the view of those who would argue about the negative impact entertainment has on society.

When Ellen Degeneres' character "came out" on the ABC sitcom *Ellen* in 1996, there was widespread concern that the TV show would encourage younger members of the audience to become lesbians. That sounds ridiculous, but it was a much-talked-about topic for religious conservatives. I recall verbally battling with many listeners on talk radio who were honestly concerned that the presence of a gay character on primetime television would actually lead to an increase in homosexuality. And as I write this book years later, there is absolutely no evidence of any increase in the gay and lesbian population in America.

It is interesting to note that those who make such bold predictions about the anticipated negative effect a particular television show, movie, song, or advertising is going to have on a mass audience never admit their mistake when the predictions are proven to be completely inaccurate.

During the presidential campaign of 1988, Vice President Dan Quayle proved that he did not understand the role of mass media and its relationship with society. It's one thing for a vice presidential candidate to misspell the word "potato," but quite another thing for a vice presidential candidate to demonstrate that he does not comprehend the relationship between mass media and society is outright scary!

During the campaign of 1988, vice presidential candidate Quayle criticized the sitcom *Murphy Brown* after it was announced that Candace Bergen's character, Murphy Brown, was planning to have a child out of wedlock as a single woman. The concern from Quayle and the conservative right was that the sitcom's content would send the message to young females that it was okay to have children out of wedlock.

The number of babies born to single women has actually decreased since 1988, yet Dan Quayle and the conservatives who agreed with his stance have still not admitted their prediction was wrong.

As a TV program, *Murphy Brown* was not attempting to encourage young girls to have babies without a father. In an ideal world, every child would have two parents. By 1988, women had become even more independent. There was a growing sense that it was unfair for society to require a male partner in order to bear a child. That trend was one of the ultimate manifestations of the Women's Lib Movement, which gained momentum in the '70s.

Think of the media, whether news or entertainment, as society's mirror. A mirror only has the ability to reflect, that which is looking into it. If there is to be any criticism of the content of the media, the criticism should fall on whatever is creating the reflection in the mirror. In this case, it is our society.

The media *reflect* a changing society

A growing acceptance of homosexuality in the real world will lead to further recognition of homosexuality in mainstream media. The alleged effects of the increasing representation of gays and lesbians in mainstream entertainment parallel the ongoing debate over the effects of violent and sexual entertainment on society.

If violent and sexual entertainment actually had the power to cause an increase in violence and sexual activity in society, then it is reasonable to believe that there would be much more violence and sex, considering the millions and millions of young people exposed to this type of entertainment every day.

The violence and degradation of women so prevalent in rap music videos, for example, has been blamed for *causing* the violence and disrespect for women among young African American males. The truth is that rap lyrics and videos have always *reflected* the violent behavior and attitudes that have long been an unfortunate part of life in many urban areas of America.

From music videos on MTV to the NBC sitcom, *Friends,* sexual content has been blamed for influencing teenagers to become sexually active. Are music videos and *Friends* inspiring teenagers to become sexually active, or do music videos, TV shows like *Friends,* and other forms of entertainment *reflect* the attitudes and actions of a young mass audience? Teenagers have always had a sense of their own sexuality and perhaps even the desire to become sexually active long before radio and television even existed. Past generations of teens did not go the barn to have sex in the hay because of any influence from mass media.

Adults now blame the media for encouraging their children to do the very things they did when they were teenagers. When today's establishment was young, the media was never used as an excuse

132

for negative behavior. If we can agree that music videos, TV shows, music, movies, and video games are essentially products that are marketed, then an understanding of contemporary marketing concepts would be helpful in better understanding why violent and sexual entertainment is so prevalent.

Entertainment: a product

Today's consumers are different. The attitude of the new consumer transcends age, race, religion, gender, or nationality. Consumers today are different from the consumers of the past. Listeners to talk and music radio, viewers of TV programming and movies, and players of video games are all consumers.

The creative artists and producers of entertainment have no agenda to turn heterosexuals into homosexuals or to turn honorable teenagers into violent criminals or sexually active animals. Hollywood has absolutely no agenda to promote homosexuality, sex or violence. The goal of any entertainment medium is to attract an audience and not change behavior. Admittedly, there are many creators of entertainment in Hollywood who would like the country to share their liberal political and social ideology, but converting audiences is not the ultimate goal of entertainment.

The new consumers today are *"seeking authenticity in most of their major purchases, whether of products, services or experiences,"* according to David Lewis author of <u>*The Soul of the New Consumer*</u>. Lewis' book is about marketing and advertising, but the observations apply equally to the general motivation behind the creation of all forms of entertainment. Lewis writes, *"The focus of some commercials* [or TV shows, movies, music, and radio] *has also shifted to portraying 'real life' characters in 'real life' surroundings to permit a greater sense of empathy between viewer and viewed."*

The entertainment industry is reacting to today's "new consumer" by more realistically reflecting society. The reason gay characters and teens interested in sex appear in entertainment simply reflects that reality in society. Echoing the observations of David Lewis, Marc Gobe' writes in his book, <u>*Emotional Branding*</u>, *"Honesty is expected. Trust is engaging and intimate."* One of the prevailing themes in current books on marketing is the new understanding that the new consumer demands honesty and authenticity. Let's face it, we've all been hyped enough! The only responsibility of the entertainment industry is to entertain and attract an audience, which is best accomplished through realism.

It's the money, stupid!

The liberals in Hollywood create movies for financial gain, with few exceptions. Steven Spielberg produced *Schindler's List* for the sole purpose of telling the story of the plight of Jews under the regime of Hitler. Ironically, the motivation to expose a truth and the realistic ambience of the movie were so compelling that it yielded great financial rewards. But that was not the motivation.

There is no conspiracy by the liberals of Hollywood to feature gay characters with the intent of changing America's collective opinion of homosexuality. Grant it, the liberals of Hollywood would prefer greater acceptance of homosexuality, but that is not their intention for creating entertainment that includes an acceptable view of gays and lesbians.

The foremost motivation of those who create entertainment is **money**. For decades, the conservative right has been complaining that Hollywood is trying to push a liberal agenda. Political and social liberals may dominate the entertainment industry, but money and power are the goals that drive Hollywood-not the advancement of an agenda.

It is understandable that liberals in the entertainment industry want to create entertainment that is reflective of their personal views, which would include gay rights, but that is not unique to liberals. The conservative right blatantly uses conservative radio talk hosts, state legislatures, Congress, the President, and the Bible in hopes of changing the collective opinions of Americans. The conservative right's accusations that liberals in Hollywood produce entertainment for the purpose of convincing America to think and act a certain way reflects their growing paranoia of the alleged "liberal media."

The entertainment and news media are not as liberal as you have been led to believe. Repeat a lie often enough and it becomes a fact. Right-wing conservatives have been so dedicated to labeling the media "liberal," that they have failed to recognize how the media have changed.

The idea of the **liberal media** has been built up to be this myopic monster that penetrates the brains of innocent and impressionable Americans who obviously cannot think for themselves. For years, there have been cries from conservatives that a liberal media has been spreading liberal propaganda and undermining the conservative voice. Most conservatives would argue that a liberal media is responsible for forcing a gay agenda on America.

In his book *What Liberal Media?* author Eric Alterman writes, *"The myth of the 'liberal media' empowers conservatives to control debate in the United States to the point where liberals cannot even hope for a fair shake anymore."* Alterman makes a strong case *against* the general belief that mass media is controlled by liberals who are dedicated to using news and entertainment to advance a liberal agenda. Shut the mantra "liberal media" out of your mind for a moment and consider a few changes.

The Fox News Channel defines its news and programming as "fair and balanced," yet any person with a pulse should be able to interpret the obvious conservative slant FNC feeds its audience. And the Fox News Channel presents conservative bias twenty-four hours a day, seven days a week.

Roger Ailes, who was instrumental in the re-election of Ronald Reagan in 1984, is the guiding light of the Fox News Channel. When Reagan fell behind Walter Mondale in the polls during the '84 Presidential Campaign, Ailes was brought in to resurrect the Reagan campaign. The rest is history. Roger Ailes has been conspicuously reluctant to remind or inform the public that the man behind the "fair and balanced" Fox News Channel is a hardcore Republican. That knowledge would greatly diminish the credibility of the "fair and balanced" image of FNC.

With few exceptions, the Fox News Channel anchors and show hosts present a strongly conservative bias on the air. The show, *No Spin Zone* hosted by Bill O'Reilly is largely conservative with some differing views emanating from O'Reilly. For example, **conservative** Bill O'Reilly *supports* gay marriage!

Conservative author Ann Coulter signed on with MSNBC in 1996 as a political analyst. She has also been a frequent guest on the Fox News Channel. Coulter is a striking blonde who is articulate and a hardcore conservative. George Will, a strong conservative, has been an integral part of ABC's Sunday morning news show as long as I can remember.

There are numerous conservative programs and conservative hosts and guests all over television. Conservative talk dominates talk radio across the country. The news media, not just the Fox News Channel, is much more "fair and balanced" than conservatives are willing to recognize. The complaint that the conservative voice is not heard because of a **liberal bias** is the result of conservative brainwashing.

The news media has never been totally fair or objective. It just isn't possible. The major networks and the major cable news channels all have hosts, reporters, and assignment editors who carry their own political bias with them to work every day. Some may actually try to be fair, but it is impossible to suppress one's strong political beliefs when covering a story about a politician or a politically charged issue. Even if it's subtle, reporters and news anchors will reveal a liberal or conservative slant, even if only by the way something is worded or by the carefully selected video that accompanies the story.

Words and phrases can be clues that reveal a reporter's political bias. Accessing body language, tone of voice, and the questions asked are also clues about political orientation. But the most important point is that anchors, reporters, and assignment editors all have political biases. It is the responsibility of the audience to understand how bias is impossible to conceal. The problem emerges when mass audiences accept, as objective, the slanted rhetoric of Rush Limbaugh or Dan Rather without understanding that personal political bias is part of the content.

The individuals who become the people of the media have their own established views on political and social issues. Our views on political and social issues become part of what we are as human beings. We navigate through life using the political and social senses we have developed. Even if biases happen in subtle ways, they still happen. The simple decision to cover one story over another is an easy way of inadvertently revealing political bias.

In an interview with President George W. Bush on NBC's *Meet the Press,* which aired on Sunday, February 8, 2004, host Tim Russert strongly challenged the president, which caused Russert to be perceived by many Americans watching as a staunch liberal. NBC's Tim Russert had been viewed as an extremely balanced interviewer who never really displayed a strong left or a strong right bias. But in that 2004 interview with President Bush in the Oval Office, Russert seemed to attack the president from a liberal perspective.

A number of TV political commentators were shocked by Russert's apparent liberal slant in the interview with President Bush. Russert's demeanor also surprised the White House. It is rare for a sitting president to agree to a one-on-one interview with someone in the media, including national media figures. You can be sure that Tim Russert was granted the interview with Bush because of Russert's perceived political fairness while conducting interviews.

It's a little-known fact that administrations control the reporters who cover presidents. For example, if a network reporter goes too far in criticizing the president and his policies, the White House will threaten to shut the reporter and their network out of the loop when it comes to important news scoops.

If an administration is not happy with the way a particular reporter is pressing the president, the direct implication is that the reporter will be the last to receive any important news from the White House, while all of the competitors will have the stories. Reporters have the right to be negative, but if a line is crossed, the reporter is shut out.

So why was Tim Russert different in the interview with Bush from the Oval Office? Russert did not suddenly change his political ideology. As host of the legendary NBC news show, *Meet the Press*, all eyes were on Russert and how he would handle the interview with Bush.

If Russert had not been tough on the president with his questioning, viewers and network peers would have criticized him for throwing "soft ball questions" at the president as a gesture for being granted the interview. Russert may have gone against his own instincts in the way he challenged Bush, but Russert did the right thing by appearing to be an adversary rather than a lapdog. He had no choice. Russert's approach to the interview reveals how the news media often takes an adversarial position just to give the impression of maintaining the image of challenging the political establishment. It was the adversarial position that created a conflict between Russert and Bush and conflict is a key element in entertainment.

Newspapers and news magazines fall victim to the same tendencies. If an editor is liberal or conservative he/she has the option of choosing pictures of politicians from a large selection. Countless photos are taken of presidential candidates during every public appearance. The photos capture a variety of facial expressions. Numerous times during the 2004 Presidential Campaign I would notice a picture of George W. Bush with a stupid expression on his face next to a more flattering picture of John Kerry. Yet, there may be a question about a photographer's ability to capture George W. Bush *not* looking stupid!

The **Media Studies Center** did a study, which showed that 89 percent of the journalists in Washington voted for Bill Clinton. The media may be made up of a greater number of liberals than conservatives, but that does not necessarily mean that the news media goes to great extremes to present a liberal bias for personal reasons.

William Bennett, former member of Bush, Sr.'s cabinet, appears on countless cable news shows. Bennett is an ultra-conservative Republican. If liberals controlled the media elites, why would a conservative like Bennett get so many opportunities to give the Republican point of view?

To promote her book, *Slander*, conservative Ann Coulter appeared on the *Today Show*, CNN's *Crossfire*, MSNBC's *Hardball*, Fox's *The Big Story with John Gibson*, along with TV shows and radio talk shows across the country. Coulter was featured in articles in *Newsday*, the *New York Observer*, and the *New York Times*.

In 2002, ABC hired Ann Coulter to be a political analyst. Referring to the news media in America, Coulter is quoted as saying, *"American journalists commit mass murder without facing the ultimate penalty, I think they are retarded."* That sounds like a conservative having an open opportunity to voice her conservative opinion on what is constantly labeled the "liberal media." And did you take note of the viciousness of Coulter's words? That bitch should be criticized for using the phrase *"commit mass murder,"* when describing the actions of American journalists! If the media really were liberal to the point of controlling news content, which is what many Americans believe, then one would think those liberals would not have given Coulter many opportunities to voice her opinions.

On CNN's *Crossfire*, a conservative commentator is on one side of the desk and one side of the issue and a liberal commentator is on the other side, physically and politically. Both sides get equal time to interview guests and to give their biased opinions on the issues. The liberal and conservative viewpoints are generally equal.

One of the most popular programs on cable is the Fox News Channel's *Hannity and Colmes.* Sean Hannity, an ultra-conservative, and liberal Alan Colmes, battle over the top political issues of the day.

The Fox News Channel is driven by a conservative slant, which is obvious in every one of its news shows. Even the format of *Hannity and Colms* reflects the conservative bias of FNC.

Sean Hannity, the conservative, is placed on the **left** side of the set with Alan Colmes, the liberal on the **right**. Their physical positioning on the set is contrary to their political ideology, but the conservative position represented by Hannity has a more dominant image because we read beginning at the left. That's the more powerful position on the set. Colmes, the liberal, is on the right side of the set which is the less dominate position.

Alan Colmes never presents a stronger argument than Sean Hannity and that is not by chance. Colmes is a frail-looking liberal who constantly fails to successfully counter Hannity's opinions. The Fox News Channel could certainly find a stronger liberal to battle Hannity, but that would not ensure that the conservative opinion would always be the more dominate opinion. Oh, but the Fox News Channel is "fair and balanced!"

Compare that to the CNN *Crossfire* set, which has always positioned the liberal on the left side of the set and the conservative on the right. Sometimes the most subconscious things are calculated ways to project subtle bias. As a viewer, listener, or reader, do not allow yourself to be oblivious to the manipulation of the media.

The aforementioned examples of the well-represented presence of conservative views in the news media should lead to the conclusion that the conservative mantra of a "liberal media" is actually a myth. Most consumers of mass media are selective in their listening, viewing, and reading. We are all guilty of focusing on only the information that supports our opinions. We are not honestly in search of an objective view. On countless occasions I have had people listening to my talk show accuse me of saying something they only *thought* I had said. They heard what they wanted to hear.

Contrary to popular belief, we tend to seek those who reflect our opinions, rather than exposing ourselves to total objectivity in the media. Those with a conservative ideology innately tune into the Fox News Channel because it supports their point-of-view.

Conservatives are less likely to spend much time watching CNN or MSNBC, two news networks that do not cater to conservative ideology. We don't want to hear the "other side" as much as we want affirmation of our opinions. This may be an indication that most of us are actually insecure with what we believe; therefore we look for others who support our opinions.

Gays in the spotlight!
"I don't care if people are gay, but why do they have to shove it my face?"

How often have you heard that question asked? Heterosexuals actually do have a legitimate reason for thinking the gay community is publicly promoting their lifestyle. But this is a false impression of the gay community. So, where did this false impression come from?

The general perception many heterosexuals have of how gays and lesbians act and react in the real world has been formed by images from television news coverage of events like gay pride parades, Mardi Gras in New Orleans, or the annual Fantasy Festival in Key West, Florida.

TV news cameras instinctively focus on the most flamboyant and outrageous homosexuals. Since many anti-gay heterosexuals have no other point of reference by which to judge homosexuals, TV images of gays and lesbians in the real world form a general impression of homosexual behavior. This unrealistic image of homosexual behavior that reaches the masses is not the manifestation of malicious intent on the part of the news media. It is the result of the nature of news.

News is entertainment! This is a realization I have come to understand after years of being in radio and television and studying mass media and its relationship with the audiences it attracts. Most of the people who work in radio and TV news do not accept news as entertainment because that suggests the news is not important or serious.

My description of news as entertainment is not criticism of the news media, rather recognition of a reality unbeknownst to the great majority of the consumers of news and those who report it daily.

Surprisingly, the vast majority of the people who populate the news media have little or no understanding of its relationship with the society it serves. Those who consume mass media daily have even less insight into the role mass media plays in their lives. The majority of those I have worked with who actually control the content of broadcast news, rarely consider the role of mass media in the real world.

As I sat in a communication theory class at Loyola University in New Orleans I began to understand the relationship between mass media and society. After several years in radio, I had a chance to take some communication classes at Loyola. I recall the communication theory professor presenting an idealistic version of the role radio and television play in society. Already in the business, I knew the professor was not teaching from a realistic point of view.

There is an old saying that *"those who can, do and those who can't, teach."* It's sad, but in many cases it's true. Teaching is a most honorable profession and most teachers are motivated to teach, not for fame or money, but for the love of teachings. However, a music professor can teach a student how to *play* music, but not how to make a hit record. And the same applies to many who teach about mass media.

If some professors and those actually in the business of mass media lack a true understanding of the relationship between media and society, how could anyone expect the general population to understand it? If the news media is to be charged with manipulating the audience, the audience is also guilty for allowing that to happen.

The image many people in this country have of gays and lesbians is based on the instinctive tendency of the news media to focus only on the most sensational aspects of any story. Gays and lesbians are not trying to *shove their lifestyle in anyone's face*! Since news *is* entertainment it is governed by the same principles that govern any form of entertainment.

Entertainment is entertaining because it takes us beyond the boundaries of ordinary life. A gay male couple that is not obviously homosexual is not as "entertaining" as a couple of drag queens displaying outrageous homosexual behavior in a gay pride parade.

Most homosexuals do not visually project their sexual orientation. They blend into society. Gays and lesbians who have careers, life partners, dogs, cats, and live quietly in their neighborhood are that the ones who are going to attract media attention. However, the flamboyant drag queens or the aggressive gay rights activists will attract news coverage. If the very nature of news is to attract attention, then it is understandable why news always focuses on outrageous behavior. Many Americans only have that point of reference for judging the homosexual community.

Do any of us want to be labeled by the news media that is interested in capturing the most compelling images in order to attract an audience?

Chapter 7

Right-wing talk radio and gay rights

WARNING: **what you learn in this chapter may alarm you!**

The Beatles happened to appear at the right moment in history and so did Rush Limbaugh. Rush Limbaugh has been credited with actually *creating* the conservative movement in the '80s. While many "dittoheads" (Rush's devout listeners) will deny this to their grave, Rush Limbaugh *did not* make America more conservative.

His conservative radio talk show gained national attention in the late '80s, which was during the second term of the Reagan administration. Limbaugh's right-wing radio show was unique at the time. His "message" hit America at a time when the lives of Baby Boomers were changing as a result of their growing affluence and exodus to the suburbs.

As the Boomer generation began making more money it collectively reacted to the image of "tax and spend Democrats." Many of those who had been Democrats were interested in holding on to more of their income. This was an invitation to explore a different political ideology.

Moving to the suburbs en masse was another power factor in the shifting attitudes of the Baby Boomers. The ambiance of the suburbs inspires more individualism, compared to life in the city, which understandably inspires more of a collective problem-solving attitude. One of the foundations of conservative ideology is individualism. The structure of the suburbs invites an "individual mentality," which then creates the growth of conservatism. It was during the early- to mid-'80s that a natural trend introduced many former liberals to conservative ideology.

It is delusional to believe that Rush Limbaugh *created* the conservative movement in the '80s. Limbaugh's radio show became the voice for the conservative movement, which was already established before his show began to gain national attention. Rather than creating the tide, Rush Limbaugh rode the tide.

Limbaugh still deserves credit for the innovative direction in which he steered talk radio. At the time Limbaugh began his radio show in Sacramento, California, there was no strong-willed right-wing talk show host attracting attention. That is hard to believe while scanning the AM radio dial today. Today's young generations that will have only known talk radio as the **"conservative media."**

Beginning in the late '80s, Rush Limbaugh's radio show was nationally syndicated and growing in popularity. By the early '90s, Limbaugh's show was considered to be a strong political force in America. The success of Rush inspired countless talk show hosts across the country to imitate his political slant and right-wing passion. The success of Limbaugh's radio show was the answer to what had always been perceived to be the **"liberal media."**

The major TV news networks, the cable channels, the network news, and the news media in general, were all charged with filtering the news and programming through a liberal perspective. Frustrated by the dominant liberal views emanating from the mainstream media, Rush Limbaugh's radio show gave conservatives their first real mainstream rebuttal to liberal views. At that time, the news media was not as politically balanced as it is today.

While his fans revered him as a political messiah, Limbaugh was honest about his true role in the political arena, at least in the early years. Limbaugh pushed aside any consideration of accepting a leadership role in the Republican Party. In his book, *HOT AIR: All Talk All the Time*, author Howard Kurtz writes that Limbaugh himself admitted his conservative slant of politics was his *"shtick."* *"I'm not out to save the country,"* was a quote from Rush Limbaugh in 1989. That was about the time his nationally syndicated talk show was rapidly building an audience. By his own admission, Limbaugh said, *"I'm out to get a large audience, I'm an **entertainer** first and a **conservative** second."* Those words came from Limbaugh himself, but I'm sure a great majority of his audience considers him a **conservative** first.

Rush Limbaugh has built his career on criticizing *every* aspect of being a Democrat or a liberal, almost to the point of implying that simply being a Democrat or a liberal is innately evil. Rush has even dismissed all "moderates" as people who have no strong conviction about political and social issues. He's wrong. Moderates usually have strong convictions about issues, but what makes them "moderate" is a willingness to view each political or social issue independent of a myopic perspective.

Limbaugh has often preached about the "loose" morals of the Democrats, including greater tolerance of drug use in America. In his condemnation of liberal ideology, Limbaugh and many conservatives promote conservative ideology as if it were more virtuous and righteous. A constant theme with Limbaugh and many other conservative radio talk show hosts is the idea that simply being a Republican or a conservative suggests greater morality. And while he publicly condemned others for their lack of virtues and honesty, Rush Limbaugh was addicted to powerful painkillers, which he allegedly purchased illegally. He had also been lying to his wife about his addiction for years.

Rush *pops*!

If Limbaugh's name had not been discovered during an investigation into the illegal sale of the painkillers Oxycotin and Vicodin in Palm Beach, Florida, we can assume he would still be popping pills today. It was rumored that Limbaugh was illegally purchasing as many as 4,000 pills every three months. Do the math. If he was purchasing 4,000 pills every three months that means Rush Limbaugh could have been using up to 1,333 pills every month-that's an average of forty-four pills a day!

Compare that to the serious addiction to Vicodin that caused Green Bay Packers' quarterback Bret Favre to check himself into rehab. Favre admitted that he had become to Vicodin and was taking about thirteen pills a day. Could the righteous and moral

Rush Limbaugh have been taking forty-three pills a day and lying to his wife about it? Imagine if a Democrat on Capitol Hill had been caught in that situation? We would still be hearing Limbaugh ranting and raving about the lack of moral values among the Democrats!

Limbaugh had become addicted to Oxycotin, a relatively new and extremely powerful painkiller. Oxycotin is essentially synthetic morphine and is prescribed to patients suffering from the most severe and chronic pain. According to his story, Limbaugh was first introduced to painkillers years ago when he was suffering from back pain. But Limbaugh so enjoyed the sensation he continued popping painkillers. Limbaugh can argue that his back has been a constant source of pain, but that's no excuse. I say that because of my personal story about my addiction to painkillers.

I have had five surgeries on the same knee, an appendectomy and radical surgery on my lower tract; I'll leave it at that. For years, I convinced one doctor after another that I needed something for chronic pain. My knee, in particular, has been a source of chronic pain even to this day. I always felt justified in asking for painkillers.

Since my career has led me to several different cities, I would convince a doctor in every new city that I had chronic knee pain, which I did, and I would get a prescription, usually for Vicodin or Ultram. Ironically, Ultram was originally promoted as a new painkiller that was not addictive. About the time I was developing my addiction, studies showed that Ultram was just as addictive as other painkillers. By that time I was already addicted.

Over a ten-year period, I was taking some kind of painkiller daily, just like Rush Limbaugh-just not as many! My addiction was mild by addiction standards. But an addiction is an addiction and if I went a day without taking a painkiller, I began to suffer withdrawal.

Following the radical surgery on my lower tract, I was in such severe pain that the doctor prescribed Oxycontin, a time-release pain medication. One pill could continue to fight pain for twelve hours. Imagine taking several of those a day?

While taking Oxycontin, I had the thought that if everyone in the world, including terrorists, were on this painkiller, there would be no hate in the world. The drug brings on feelings of euphoria and extreme confidence. Unlike many other painkillers, Oxycontin provided me with energy rather than sedation. It is a wonderful drug-too wonderful, perhaps.

A few years ago, Oxycontin became the recreational drug of choice on some high school campuses. High school students would either steal the drug from senior citizens who had it for their chronic pain, or they would buy the drug from seniors who needed money more than a drug to fight pain. Several teenagers died after crushing Oxycontin pills into a powder to experience the full potency of a twelve-hour pain pill all at once.

The purpose of sharing my drug addiction story is to establish credibility in my criticism of Rush Limbaugh. One day I realized that I would never be the best that I was capable of being if I continued taking painkillers on a daily basis. So I decided to quit. I went through physical and mental hell for two weeks, but then it was over!

Criticizing liberals as a group deficient in morality and virtues while taking a large number of pain pills every day and lying to his wife, turned Rush Limbaugh into a classic hypocrite. Many of his faithful listeners made excuses for his behavior. Do you think the conservative listeners of Rush Limbaugh, the "dittoheads," would have been as understanding if shock rocker Marilyn Manson admitted he had a serious addiction to drugs?

This episode in Rush Limbaugh's life and the reaction of many of his listeners exposes the fallacy of the conservative rhetoric. Since Limbaugh and his conservative clones oppose gay marriage, I want to expose and discredit the source of conservative opposition. After criticizing Limbaugh on my radio talk show, I received an e-mail from a man who was defending his hero, Rush. In the e-mail, the man took offense when I said that Rush was addicted to drugs. The man wrote, *"the drugs Rush took were not illegal drugs, they were prescription painkillers."* I responded, *"They were illegal drugs if they were obtained illegally!"*

To further illustrate his blatant hypocrisy, Rush Limbaugh said on his show that the investigation into his alleged illegal purchasing of painkillers was politically motivated. Limbaugh accused the Democrats of a conspiracy because those leading the investigation were Democrats. Was Rush Limbaugh saying that a Democrat in a position of enforcing the law is motivated politically when the suspect is a Republican? For Rush Limbaugh to scream "left-wing conspiracy" was the ultimate hypocrisy.

Shortly after the bombing of the Federal Building in Oklahoma City in 1999, President Clinton said the hate that led to the tragic bombing was inspired by the political hate that was coming from right-wing talk radio. Limbaugh and many other talk show hosts, including myself, were quick to criticize President Clinton for suggesting that there was a "vast right-wing conspiracy" supported by conservative talk radio. But for Limbaugh to say that a "left-wing conspiracy" was responsible for the criminal investigation into his alleged illegal purchasing of painkillers was exactly what he criticized Clinton for in 1999.

When he returned to his radio show after spending five weeks in rehab, Limbaugh showed little, if any, remorse. Though a criminal investigation continued into how he obtained the painkillers, Rush returned to the air as if his reputation were so strong that it could never be tarnished. On his first day back on the air, Rush did briefly mention the five weeks he spent in rehab and his addiction to painkillers.

There is something quite satisfying about witnessing the downfall of someone who projects superiority over others. Even those who agree with his political ideology would have to recognize that Rush Limbaugh is extremely self-righteous and pious.

When ultra-conservative William Bennett was caught with a serious gambling debt as a result of a gambling addiction, many Americans relished the moment that the man who wrote _The Book of Virtues_ was exposed for lacking his _own_ virtue. I would not criticize anyone for gambling with money that does not take food off the table, but William Bennett has been a beacon for the righteous political right. The revelation of a gambling addiction and the subsequent lying to his wife about his gambling problem were victories for those who would like to expose Republicans for their self-righteous attitudes.

Limbaugh and Bennett demonstrated that conservative Republicans are not more virtuous and moral than liberals, just less honest about it.

The truth about conservative talk in America

A final thought about **the power of Rush Limbaugh.** If Limbaugh were as powerful as his audience believes and others fear, then how did Bill Clinton win the election in 1992 and re-election in 1996? Limbaugh vigorously attacked Clinton and everything he said during the campaigns, yet Clinton won both elections. If Rush Limbaugh were such a powerful political force in America, why was he unable to convince enough Americans to vote for the Republicans running against Clinton?

Contrary to what many people believe about the influence of talk radio, it is just entertainment. That's not to say that a lot of credible information and valid political insight doesn't come from talk radio shows across America, but the purpose of a radio talk show is not the dissemination of information. The purpose of a radio talk show is to attract an audience. Yet, I know talk show hosts who honestly believe it is their responsibility to change the world.

Unbeknownst to those talk show hosts, their actual role is to attract an audience. On the subject of gay marriage, conservative talk show hosts believe it is their role in society to protect the traditional institution of marriage.

If you question my statement that talk radio is entertainment—even politically oriented talk radio—then think about some of the parties you have been to recently. Did the subject of politics ever become part of conversations, probably in the kitchen? Discussions about political and social issues are an entertaining part of social events, especially after a few drinks. The conversations may contain meaningful content, but the "conversations" are a form of entertainment.

People do not go to parties with the intention of having a serious conversation about political or social issues, but the instinct of human beings encourages the acknowledgement that peers are also aware of topical news stories. It is a way of bonding in what is a society that encourages isolation. In this sense, *all* talk radio is entertainment. It is not my intent to discredit talk radio, but it is important for the listeners (the consumers) of talk radio to understand that it's all just a show!

Rush Limbaugh and most conservative talk show hosts view every political and social issue through a myopic perspective. The very strict ideological view of political and social issues does not represent the way most people judge issues. I personally know hardcore conservatives who defy the moral code of strict conservative ideology by participating in out-of-wedlock sex or by frequenting strip clubs. Most Americans do not see every political and social issue in a strictly conservative or liberal way. A conservative Republican might be pro-choice while a liberal Democrat might be pro-life.

In general, talk radio is dominated by "conservative talk," yet only about 21 percent of Americans define themselves as **conservative**, while only about 19 percent define their ideology as **liberal.** The rest are **moderates.** So the question that begs to be answered is, why is conservative talk radio so dominant?

Conservative talk radio has been highly successful for two reasons. First, the perception that the media, in general, is liberal created a need for a rebutting medium. But the primary reason for the success of conservative talk radio is the conflict that is generated from the nature of conservative ideology.

Liberals, by nature, tend to have the attitude of "you live your life and I'll live mine." Conservatives, on the other hand, have a strong desire to *force* their political, social, and religious views on the masses. It is from this desire to tell others how they should lead their lives that encourages verbal confrontations, or conflict. Conflict has been an integral element in entertainment from its earliest beginnings.

If public opinion polls show that a majority of Americans oppose legal marriage for gays and lesbians, then is seems logical that the best way to attract the biggest possible audience would be to mirror the majority opinion. Talk show hosts have the discretion to select or enhance certain opinions in response to public opinion polls. A conservative talk show host might enjoy pornography in his personal life, but oppose it on the air in order to maintain a strict moral image.

Opposition to gay marriage is aligned with the morality of conservative politics. While it might actually be congruent with conservative ideology to support gay marriage based on the concept of the power of the individual to decide vs. government intervention, conservative talk show hosts go on the air and feed their audiences what they believe their audiences wants to hear. This is not to say that the hosts, themselves, do not agree with the views they are presenting on the air. But in many cases I have personally known that certain talk show hosts have stayed away from discussing issues that are not in line with the image they have created.

As long as the goal of talk radio or the news media is to attract the largest possible audience, then talk radio and the news media will be guided by the same principles that govern any entertainment medium. While an audience may gain important facts, perspectives, or information through serious-oriented mediums, like talk radio or TV news, it is crucial for the audience to understand what motivates the media they consume daily. Even serious talk radio is entertainment.

The media's reluctance to totally embrace the crusade for gay rights, including the more extreme idea of gay marriage, is out of fear that audiences will be offended or alienated. Attracting an audience reigns supreme over saying what should be said.

The year 2004 marks a significant moment in the gay rights movement. With the debate over the right for same-sex couples to legal marriage beginning to reach critical mass, Americans will become increasingly more comfortable with the idea. As the comfort level for the further advancement of gay rights grows, the media will begin to reflect the changing attitude of the masses.

Contrary to the belief that the media dictates the behavior of the mass population, it is actually the audience that dictates the content of the media. From the local TV news to radio talk shows, it is the audience that controls the content of the various forms of entertainment through its collective support, or lack thereof. But sometimes a smaller group of listeners with an agenda can manifest change in entertainment that is popular with a large audience.

By March 2004, the Federal Communications Commission had been pressured by the growing concern that many radio talk shows, which had built a reputation on shocking sexual content, needed to be regulated by the agency. Howard Stern and Bubba the Love Sponge, an FM morning host in Tampa, were among the first victims of the FCC's new mission of cleaning up the airwaves.

Clear Channel Communications, the company that owns the most radio stations in America, cancelled Howard Stern from their stations that carried his show. Clear Channel also sent out a memo threatening immediate termination of any employee at any radio station that violated the company's new standards for decency. Every Clear Channel radio station in America held mandatory seminars for all of the employees that were involved in any aspect of programming. The seminars spelled out, in detail, the strict new rules for all Clear Channel programming.

One of the most sacred characteristics of America as a nation is the lack of government control over the media. In many nations, all media are owned and controlled by the government. Governments use their media as a propaganda tool. Concerns of a news media that is biased and an entertainment industry that is too sexually graphic and violent are minor concerns compared to the government controlling the content of entertainment.

Connecting all this to the debate over gay marriage is coming.

Chapter 8

Gays gone *wild*!

It was 1975. Rachel—my wife at the time—and I had gone on vacation to Key West, Florida. We stayed at a quaint, historic hotel named The Pier House. The first night, we had dinner in the main restaurant and as we glanced around we both noticed something we had never seen before. Rachel and I looked at each other and realized we were one of only two couples in the restaurant that appeared to be heterosexual!

Having grown up in New Orleans, I was exposed to homosexuals and drag queens every time our family went to the French Quarter. By 1975, when disco dominated the dance scene, the gay clubs in New Orleans played the hottest new disco music and were the best places to dance, even for heterosexuals. Gays dominated the clubs, but heterosexuals always felt welcome.

On that first night in the restaurant of the Pier House in Key West, it was obvious this was a resort hotel where gay men felt comfortable enough to be openly gay. As the weekend progressed it became obvious that the Pier House was actually a gay resort, or at the very least, a resort that catered to gays. Neither Rachel nor I were uncomfortable with our newly discovered surroundings, but even though we had both grown up in New Orleans, we had never experienced a hotel or resort that attracted gays and lesbians as its predominant clientele. To this day, that remains a very memorable vacation. Several years after that 1975 trip, I read that Key West had become a popular getaway for homosexuals. I wasn't surprised.

The next time I vacationed in Key West was with my girlfriend, Brenda, in 1999. By that time, Key West had become well established as a vacation destination for gays and lesbians. Consequently, I expected to be among many openly gay and lesbian couples at that beautiful spot on the planet. It is sad to think that many gays and lesbians feel safe being openly gay in a place like Key West, only to return to their closet back home.

Every summer, Key West hosts *Fantasy Fest*, which is a gay parade and celebration best described as a mini-Mardi Gras. This event now attracts many heterosexuals who realize that homosexuals know how to "party!"

As I think back on the many years I experienced Mardi Gras in the French Quarter of New Orleans, it was the uninhibited frivolity of gays and lesbians, along with their outlandish behavior and attire, that made Mardi Gras a special and quite unique experience.

It was during my last trip to Key West in 1999 that I began to realize that the homosexual community is extremely attractive to the travel industry. The average annual income of homosexuals is about $5,000 greater than the average income of heterosexuals. In addition to more disposable income, the majority of homosexuals are not homebound with children. Money and freedom make the homosexual community a gold mine to the travel industry.

However, marketing overtly to homosexuals has its negative side. Many travel destinations, be it cities or resorts, are reluctant to openly target gay men and lesbians, out of fear that fundamentalist Christians might launch a boycott in retaliation for the acceptance of homosexuals.

Every spring, Disney World in Orlando, Florida hosts *Gay Days* at the theme park. During *Gay Days* thousands of homosexuals from across the country come together for a show of unity and a great time at Disney World. But this annual migration of gays and lesbians has not gone unnoticed by the Religious Right. Many religious conservatives have *demanded* that Disney stop allowing the mass influx of homosexuals to the theme park every spring.

The controversy is based on the idea that the presence of homosexuals at Disney World destroys the theme park's purity and child-friendly image. During *Gay Days* it is common to see gay male couples and lesbian couples holding hands and generally showing the same signs of affection heterosexual couples display in public.

Disney continues to welcome homosexuals for *Gay Days*. Disney was also one of the first corporations in America to extend benefits to domestic partners. Too many companies bow to threats from special interest groups, like the Religious Right, Disney should be applauded for standing firm by its beliefs.

Those who oppose further acceptance of homosexuality have complained that the mere sight of gay males and lesbians walking hand-in-hand is inappropriate for the many children who might witness the activity. Answering their children's questions about two men or two women acting like a heterosexual couple in love is something many parents do not wish to face.

Today, parents want to ban anything that might cause their children to ask questions about certain uncomfortable topics. Yet, by simply answering the questions of their children parents would better prepare their children for the real world that awaits them.

And what *about* these questions children might be asking? Are parents not capable of addressing the curious questions of their children? What about the point that parents should not be put in a position to answer such questions?

Many younger children would probably not even ask questions about same-sex couples, unless, of course, their parents went to drastic measures to shield their children from the sight of homosexuals. And if not at *Gay Days* at Disney, *everyone's* children will see a gay male or lesbian couple somewhere, maybe even in the local Wal-Mart. Interesting that Wal-Mart is not a gay-friendly corporation until it comes time for homosexuals to spend money in their stores!

So how should a parent answer a child's question about homosexuals in public? Here's one example: A male child sees a male couple and asks his mother, *"Mommy, why are those two men holding hands?"* The mother replies, *"Son, Daddy and I love each other and we are a couple. Do you understand that?"* *"Sure,"* says the son. Mom continues, *"Well, sometimes two men or two women fall in love the same way and become a couple."* To which the son would probably reply, *"Can we get some candy now?"*

It is not difficult for parents to explain male or female couples to their children, but here's the problem. Parents have the tendency to view the world through the eyes of their children, but with their own adult life experiences. For example, if a child asked why two men were walking with their arms around each other and the mother said, *"Don't look at that! Those men are sinners and will burn in hell. God does not want two men or two women to ever be together,"* naturally the child would become extremely curious about same-sex couples.

When it comes to answering questions about homosexuality, children do not need to be told about the sexual aspect of the lifestyle. Children only need the information that is appropriate for their level of comprehension. Their questions should gage how much needs to be explained. If children learned at an early age about the reality that some men and women fall in love with a person of the same gender, condemnation of homosexuality could be wiped out in our lifetime. Maybe that's the fear of anti-gay parents?

Homosexuals have more money

One of the reasons Disney refuses to bend under pressure from Christian groups that continue to demand an end to *Gay Days* is the company's sense of fairness; but also because the homosexual community has great financial resources.

The gay travel business has become a $54-billion-a-year industry and gay travel accounts for about 10 percent of the total industry. Sadly, there are many cities that are popular tourist destinations, yet will never advertise to the gay community out of fear of a backlash from the conservative right. But many other cities are boldly opening their arms to gay and lesbian travelers.

In 1991, Richard Gray opened the Royal Palms Hotel, a thirteen-unit property, in Ft. Lauderdale, Florida. The hotel began attracting primarily gay males. One of the main selling points was the *ten-man* hot tub and lavender-scented towels. In the swimming pool, swimsuits were optional! When the Royal Palms opened in 1991, it was the *only* gay-oriented resort destination in Ft. Lauderdale. By the end of 2003, there were thirty!

In the December 8, 2003 edition, the *USA Today* featured an article titled; **"Cities come out about wooing gays—and their dollars."** The article reported on the growing number of cities that were using advertising dollars to attract gay and lesbian travelers. Would you expect the city of Bloomington, Indiana to be a destination for homosexuals?

Bloomington adopted the slogan, **"Come Out and Play,"** and simply added rainbow colors to the logo. The slogan was an open invitation to gays and lesbians that they were welcome in Bloomington.

New Haven, Connecticut issued a brochure promoting their slogan, **"Your Alternative Getaway."** In the spring of 2004, Philadelphia began airing TV commercials that directly targeted gays and lesbians. One slogan for Philadelphia was, **"Get your history straight and your nightlife gay."** The "City of Brotherly, and now Sisterly Love" has run an ad showing Benjamin Franklin flying a rainbow-colored kite. Philadelphia spends about $300,000 per year to attract homosexual visitors.

The nation's capitol has created a gay-friendly slogan, **"Where More Than Just the Cherry Blossoms Come Out,"** in hopes of tapping into the lucrative gay travel market. Miami, Portland, Oregon, Minneapolis, San Diego, and Palm Springs, California have all promoted their cities as gay-friendly vacation destinations.

But not every city is willing to openly advertise for homosexual travelers. Dallas, Atlanta, and Chicago have yet to commit to a gay-friendly advertising campaign out of the fear that protests would come from the religious fundamentalists surrounding those big cities.

One of the hot vacations spots for gays and lesbians for Memorial Day weekend is Pensacola, Florida. Every year about 60,000 gays and lesbians "party" in that city with sugar fine, snow-white beaches and warm, aqua-colored Gulf waters. Pensacola has a gay community, but the city is located at the western part of the Florida panhandle, about 45 minutes from the Alabama border. This is a very conservative part of the country that has an active population of Christian fundamentalists. I know—I lived there!

Pensacola was the city in which Christian fundamentalist Paul Hill, the father of four young children murdered an abortion doctor as the doctor entered his clinic. Explain to me how a Christian can be pro-life but end the life of another human being?

Paul Hill was executed by lethal injection in 2003 for his conviction on first-degree murder charges. A pro-life activist had to be killed because he killed. How ironic. I wonder if Paul Hill felt that leaving four young children without their father was the Christian thing to do?

In 2004, about 660,000 gays and lesbians traveled to the Ft. Lauderdale, generating nearly $600 million in revenue. That accounted for 12 percent of Ft. Lauderdale's annual tourism. That demonstrates that homosexuals travel and spend more money per capita than heterosexuals.

The Census Bureau does not ask about sexual orientation when taking a census. But in the 2000 census, 1.2 million people reported living together as same-sex partners. So how many homosexuals are there in America? It's impossible to know for sure. Gay activists promote that gays and lesbians make up 10 percent of the U.S. population. Others believe the real number is closer to 3 percent.

Considering the number of homosexuals who are concerned about revealing their sexual orientation, it may be more realistic to assume that about 5 percent of the US population is homosexual. If the homosexual population is about 5 percent of the total population but accounts for about 10 percent of the travel market, cities and resorts are wise to advertise directly to gays and lesbians.

The cities that have openly targeted gay and lesbian tourists have not gone unnoticed. In an article in *USA Today,* Robert Knight, director of the Culture and Family Institute is quoted saying, *"They're worshipping at the altar of money, and they couldn't care less what God might think, or how it might impact children."* I have to agree with Knight's concern that advertising campaigns targeting homosexual travelers might have an impact on children. These advertising campaigns might just teach children that homosexuality is a normal part of our society. And consider how much revenue is generated from gay and lesbian travelers. Many cities are broke or nearly broke and sales tax revenue relieves some of the tax burden from the citizens of cities.

Knight went on to say, *"They* (the cities) *promote homosexuality as if it's harmless. And that is not the case."* What research or statistics could Mr. Knight reveal that would support his assumption?

There should be more challenges to statements about the acceptance of homosexuality "hurting children" or "harming society." There is no justification for the argument that the sexual relationships between consenting adults in private will have a negative impact on children or harm society. Unless, of course, adults explain the details of homosexual sex to children before they are mentally prepared to process such information.

Would the religious adults who condemn homosexuality explain the details of heterosexual sex at an age when the child is not ready for the information? Open acceptance of homosexuality and the recognition of gay marriage will have *no* adverse effects on children or society.

There are creative ways to subtly advertise to gays and lesbians without causing a stir with religious fundamentalists. A perfect example is a TV commercial for the on-line travel service Orbitz, which aired regularly on network and cable television in 2003.

The commercial featured old-style puppets with disproportionate heads and obvious strings. The commercial was a take-off on a 1950s TV show about space travel. In the Orbitz commercial, one of the male puppets is in charge of a retro, space-age control room, where he makes travel arrangements for Orbitz customers.

One of the commercials shocked me in a positive way. Travel arrangements had been made at a beachfront hotel for a male and female couple. The man and the woman were on the balcony overlooking the beach, the ocean, and the pool. The woman said something about how nice the view was from their balcony. The man, using a pair of binoculars, panned down to the body of a well-toned man tanning by the pool. The man on the balcony agreed that the view was great!

It was subtle, but obvious to gays, lesbians, and metrosexuals that the man on the balcony was focused on the guy tanning by the pool. The commercial concluded with the puppet in the control room declaring that Orbitz had sent another traveler to the right spot.

Cruising for gays!

The Atlantis cruise line produces a slick brochure promoting all-gay cruises. One heading reads, **Atlantis: The Way We Play.** The brochure displays pictures of gay men and lesbians playing in the pool on the ship, relaxing in the sun, or embracing another on the deck. A Hawaiian Islands cruise was billed as **The World's Largest All-Gay Cruise aboard the Norwegian Star. The finest ship ever to sail an all-gay cruise.** Can't you imagine the people on that cruise having a lot more fun than some of the pretentious heterosexuals that go on cruises?

Criticism from the Religious Right of *Gay Days* at Disney World, *Fantasy Fest* in Key West, or cities targeting homosexual travelers will continue as part of the crusade to halt the total acceptance of gays and lesbians. Here's a thought that discredits the Religious Right. A conservative Christian who owns a business might condemn the presence of homosexuals at Disney World or Key West. He might be critical of his city for targeting gay and lesbian travelers, yet he would not be concerned with the sexual orientation of a customer that walks into his business to spend money.

Earlier in this chapter there was this quote from Robert Knight of the Culture and Family Institute about the cities in America now actively advertising for homosexual travelers: *"They're worshipping at the altar of money."* What a perfect way to describe every conservative Christian business owner in America who is critical of homosexuals, yet does business with *any* customer regardless of their sexual orientation. Those Christian business owners are aborting their convictions to "worship at the altar of money."

PART IV

Chapter 9

Metrosexuals: a new special interest group?

There is a newly invented word that describes a group of people who have never been given a collective identity. The word is **metrosexual** (n.) 1) a guy who appears as if he could be gay but is straight 2) a guy who is comfortable in gay bars and in the company of homosexuals. 3) a guy who could be friends with a lesbian without anxiously awaiting the moment he can watch her have sex with another woman!

Metrosexuals are the straight guys shopping alone at Pottery Barn or Bed, Bath, and Beyond. Metrosexual men are often mistaken for homosexuals by co-workers, friends, and even strangers. Metrosexuals are least likely to be found in redneck bars, at monster truck shows, or walking through a gun show. The simplest definition of a metrosexual is a male who is in touch with his feminine side and doesn't care!

The characteristics of being a metrosexual don't apply to women as much as men because the stigma of homosexuality is greater for men than women. Not fair-but reality.

Here's a brief test to determine if you are a metrosexual male:
1) Do you refer to a planned set of clothing as an "outfit?" (T or F)
2) Have you ever admitted that Brad Pitt or Jon Bon Jovi have nice butts? (T or F)
3) Who would you be most comfortable kissing on the lips:
   a) Hugh Grant
   b) Keanu Reeves
   c) Harrison Ford
   d) Britney Spears
4) At which clothing store are you more likely to find acceptable clothing:
   a) Army surplus store
   b) the hunting section of Target
   c) Express for Men
   d) T.J. Maxx
5) Which of the following would you prefer doing:
   a) watch a boxing match
   b) ride an ATV through mud
   c) change the oil in your car
   d) get a facial

[answers: T, T, d, c, d]

If you answered four or more questions correctly, congratulations, you are a metrosexual!

All my life, I have known I was different. I just did not fit in with guys in high school and college and I have never totally bonded with guys. Maybe I don't know how to have a "guy friend." I don't ever recall going "drinking with the guys." I have, for the most part, lived my life in a way that was congruent with my instincts, regardless of what others thought of me. I have always been repulsed by the mating techniques of the heterosexual male. It's out right embarrassing to be in their presence!

I reached a point in my life when I decided I could no long live the lie. I "came out" as a metrosexual. Admitting to friends and co-workers that I was a metrosexual was a liberating experience. However, I am ashamed to admit that I'm still concealing my metrosexual lifestyle from some family members. They just wouldn't understand. My brother and one of my sisters are born-again Christians and have raised their children to believe that God condemns homosexuality. If they ever discovered that I was a metrosexual I know they would quote that part in the Bible that condemns metrosexuality! Somewhere in Leviticus does it not state that, *"man shall not appear, in any way, to look or act like man who would lie down with man, like with woman."* Yet, in my heart, I believe God accepts me as a metrosexual.

Can we be sure Jesus was not a metrosexual? He was fashionable for the time, considerate, and very compassionate... and persecuted. All are characteristics of being a metrosexual!

Because of the social stigma associated with metrosexuality it took a lot of resolve for me to admit that to myself. It is important for metrosexuals to come to terms with who they are and to begin to live their lives openly and proudly. Many people who condemn metrosexuals believe we made a conscious decision to lead the lifestyle. That is ridiculous! Metrosexuals were born that way, yet society has caused many to be ashamed of what they are.

It is very difficult being a metrosexual in school. Every school in America should have a program that teaches all students to be tolerant and accepting of metrosexuals. There was a recent controversy over a book that was being used in several school districts to teach tolerance of metrosexuals, titled: *Bobby Has a Daddy Who Acts Like a Mommy*!

Two books changed my life forever. *He: a study of masculine psychology* and *She: a study of feminine psychology*, both written by psychologist Robert A. Johnson.

When I was coming of age, I followed the lead of the guys who were popular and always seemed to attract the pretty girls. I was conditioned to think that guys with macho attitudes were the guys who were successfully meeting and picking up girls.

The two books, *He* and *She*, were an epiphany for me! As I read, I realized that I had never been really been true to myself. I had always followed the masculine norms for men. Those two simple books by Robert A. Johnson gave me permission to accept myself for who I was, which among other things was a metrosexual!

He and *She* revealed that every man has a feminine side and every woman has a masculine side. The books also pointed out that no matter how civilized and socialized we become as a species, we will always be innately male or female. In other words, our male and female instincts are part of who we are and to deny such a significant reality is to declare war against ones self.

If a tiger, for example, were denied its instincts, the tiger would not survive in his/her environment. A man or woman's life may not be in jeopardy by the denial of instincts, but a person would not evolve into a whole and content being if natural instincts were ignored. Men will always possess an instinct to be protective of women and feel a need to provide for women. That is not sexist-it's instinct. Men have paternal instincts and woman have maternal instincts.

He and *She* taught me to acknowledge my feminine side, rather than ignore it. I gave myself permission to follow my instincts. I was never very successful at meeting girls in high school. Looking back I can appreciate that society only taught boys to be macho. It was only after reading *He* and *She* that I realized that "macho" didn't work for me and I could meet females by just being me!

Not all women are interested in guys who are in touch with their feminine side. Women who don't understand men who are in touch with their feminine side may be women who are so extremely feminine they repel against the like poles of the less macho males. Or, perhaps like me, they were conditioned to see men in only one light.

The degree to which society has condemned homosexuals has led to critical judgment of anyone who might *appear* homosexual. In the eyes of many people, any male that doesn't project testosterone-motivated behavior is believed to be gay, or now metrosexual.

Metrosexual, as a new label for men who are not afraid to be honest with their instincts, defines a group that doesn't need special rights, but the label does appropriately provide a word that accurately describes many straight guys. If you are a metrosexual you are not alone. In fact, you're in rather good company.

Here's an incomplete list of famous metrosexuals:
Kelsey Grammer
David Hyde-Pierce
Mick Jagger
Hugh Grant
Dick Van Dyke

President Bill Clinton
Steven Tyler (Aerosmith)
Jon Bon Jovi
Calvin Klein (or any fashion designer who isn't gay)
David Letterman
Keanu Reeves (if the rumors are not true, of course)
Clay Aiken (*American Idol*)
Tom Cruise
Brad Pitt

Gay backlash to meterosexuals

If the term metrosexual continues to cause a lot of guys to feel they are now defined as "straight with a feminine side," more straight guys could start going to more gay bars and nightclubs. Should that happen there is the possibility of a backlash from the homosexual community.

In an episode of the over-the-edge animated TV show *South Park,* which airs on Comedy Central, the eight-year-old kids and their fathers became metrosexuals. Mr. Garrison, the obviously gay schoolteacher, became resentful of the idea of metrosexuality.

Mr. Garrison and his friend, "Mr. Slave," a leather-clad gay guy with a collar and chain around his neck, went to the local gay bar in South Park. Since the town's fathers had become metrosexuals, they began hanging out in the gay bar. Mr. Garrison asked one of the fathers he saw in the bar, *"Would you like to go in the bathroom with me so I can give you a hand-job?"* The father was shocked and emphatically answered, *"NO!"* Mr. Garrison asked, *"Then what are you doing here?"* The obvious assumption was that men who appear to be gay and are hanging out in a gay bar must be gay! That assumption was more logical before metrosexuality.

Mr. Garrison approached another of the town's fathers and said something like, *"Hey, would you like to go home with me and Mr. Slave so you can pound Mr. Slave in the—-?* Again, that father was shocked and replied, *"NO!"* Another one of the new metrosexuals came up to Mr. Garrison and asked, *"Do these clothes make me look gay?"* To which Mr. Garrison replied, *"No, but those shoes make you look like you want to get pounded in the—-!"*

Mr. Garrison lamented about the days when the men in a gay bar were actually *gay*. As I watched that episode of *South Park* I couldn't help but think that there may be some truth to what the character was feeling. Almost every episode of *South Park* contains great wisdom about many of America's most prominent political and social issues. It would not be unusual for an episode of *South Park* contain a profound message. And that episode did.

Recently, I was with a group of people, including a lesbian, three drag queens, a straight female, and myself. We met at the newest trendy gay club in Denver. I was sitting with the group and the chair next to me was empty. A bar patron sat down and started a conversation. I did nothing that would have led him to think I was gay. A few minutes later, he was talking to the straight girl in our group and I overheard him say to her that I was cute. That's a compliment, right? She then told him that I was totally straight and had a girlfriend. Upon learning the truth, the gay guy turned to me and with a malicious tone said, *"F—- you!"*

I doubt there will be any real *metro-bashing* by gays, but a powerful bond does unite the gay community. As it stands now, the presence of heterosexuals in gay bars and gay dance clubs is seen as a form of acceptance and validation. But if the gay community begins to sense an invasion of metrosexuals, there could be a growing fear that the dynamics of their comfort zone would be threatened. And that's what would lead to a backlash.

In their book, <u>Megatrends 2000</u>, authors John Naisbitt and Patricia Aburdene explain that there is a negative aspect to America and the world growing closer and more multicultural. Naisbitt and Aburdene write, *"But even as our lifestyles grow more similar, there are unmistakable signs of a powerful countertrend: a backlash against uniformity, a desire to assert the uniqueness of one's culture and language, a repudiation of foreign influence."*

Their theory explains the future problems that could develop as a result of greater numbers of metrosexuals (straight men) becoming more prominent in the homosexual community. To further explain a culture's tendency to defend its purity, Naisbitt and Aburdene conclude, *"The more homogeneous our lifestyles become, the more steadfastly we shall cling to deeper values—religion, language, art, and literature. As our outer worlds grow more similar, we will increasingly treasure the traditions that spring from within."* In the past two decades, we have all witnessed this phenomenon in our nation and around the world.

In many ways, the attempts to create a multicultural society in America have backfired. African Americans, Caucasians, Italian Americans, Asian Americans, Native Americans, and others have found renewed pride growing their cultures. But extreme pride in ones culture is often perceived as a sign of prejudice. The compound labels of African American, Italian American, and Asian American suggest a motivation of separation. Is that pride or prejudice?

The natural desire to protect a culture in the face of an invasion of individuals and ideals from the outside could, one day, apply to the homosexual community. There is no evidence that the homosexual community feels threatened by the presence of heterosexuals, but who would have predicted that the attempts at multiculturalism in America and the world growing closer as a "global village" would have delivered a negative effect. Maybe if we are all aware of the possibility that sometime in the future homosexuals *may* feel their unity is dissolving through more assimilation in society, we can prevent it from happening.

Chapter 10

I fell in love with a lesbian!

It was the first night we had gone out together and we all had too much to drink! Her very attractive straight female friend was with us that night. I lived in a downtown loft so it was easy to suggest that they both spend the night and drive home in the morning.

This lesbian I had met was striking. She could have been a model. And here I was with an incredibly beautiful tall lesbian and her very attractive, also tall, female friend! On the assumption that "every woman is one drink away from being a lesbian," I found myself with two great-looking women who had too much to drink and they were spending the night with me!

And then it was time to go to bed!

At this point I should probably start at the beginning. And remember, I am a straight male.

Every heterosexual should have a close homosexual friend. A lesbian named Angie Lewark and I met one night in a downtown Denver bar through two cross-dressing friends we shared, Markie and Raven. There was an instant chemistry between Angie and me, which is why it was so comfortable for us to exchange phone

169

numbers that first night. A day later Angie and I had plans to have dinner. Our initial relationship was based on a simple friendship between a straight guy and a lesbian. But it didn't stay that way.

Angie is a tall, beautiful and very stylish twenty-seven-year-old lipstick-lesbian. She walks into a room with the confidence of a runway model. I'm not comfortable describing myself, but I want you to have a visual of us as a "couple." I have been told by others that I have a "modern" look, strawberry blonde hair, and a slight build at 5'7." Angie was naturally taller than I was and when she put on her sexy shoes she was suddenly much taller. Wherever we went, we were quite a striking and interesting-looking couple.

The first night Angie and I went out she was with her straight female friend, Tracy. We all had a bit too much to drink that night and I strongly suggested that they both spend the night at my apartment and drive home in the morning. A lesbian and a straight girl spending the night in a straight guy's loft? This was the stuff fantasies are made of! Since this is not erotic fiction but reality, I am compelled to tell you *exactly* what happened that night.

Once back at my apartment there wasn't even a question as to who was going to sleep where. It all happened as if it were part of our nightly routine.

Angie's straight friend, Tracy, slept on my sofa. Angie and I slept together in my bed. It felt so natural, but we knew it wasn't natural for a straight guy and a lesbian to jump in bed together after going out for the first time. How did Angie know I wasn't one of those straight guys who would have used the opportunity to try to have sex with a lesbian? Having sex with this beautiful twenty-seven-year-old lesbian, who had *never* been with a man, would have been like having sex with a virgin who knew all the moves!   Or I could have been one of those egotistical straight guys who think sex with them would suddenly cause a lesbian to be sexually attracted to men!

Regardless of how perfect this opportunity was for attempting to do what so many men can only dream of-Angie and I hugged in bed as we fell asleep. It was actually a touching memory both of us will hold forever.

The next morning the sofa was empty. Angie's straight friend had gone home before the two of us woke up. So we were now alone. How many times do you find yourself waking up with someone you had only gone out with once? All right, we all know the answer to that so perhaps I should phrase it another way! Waking up with a person you have only been out with once can be extremely uncomfortable. You are no longer under the influence of alcohol and those first moments of waking are very personal, and not just from an appearance standpoint. My new lesbian friend and I had every reason to feel uncomfortable, but we didn't.

Angie didn't want to wear the sexy, rather revealing black top she had worn to the clubs the night before, so I had given her one of my T-shirts to sleep in. She did sleep in her pants, by the way.

Although Angie shared the same basic features and mannerism of an ex-girlfriend I had lived with and had a very passionate relationship with, I never once thought of a potential sexual relationship with my new lesbian friend. While Angie is stunningly attractive, I respected her sexual orientation. Most straight guys I know would have at least *attempted* to introduce the idea of sex.

A number of my straight male friends have seen Angie and *every* one said at some point "I'd love to ---- her!" Hell, even my straight female friends have said that!

My feelings toward Angie gave me a completely new sensation. There was something else I didn't know about her at this point. I didn't know whether or not she occasionally had sex with men. I knew that some homosexuals occasionally have sex with heterosexuals.

While I never bonded closely with guy friends, I never had difficulty bonding with women. Angie was *perfect!* She was a girl and it appeared she was becoming a friend. The day after we spent the night together, Angie and I talked on the phone about as often as two people headed for an emotional and sexual relationship would. Within a couple of days we had gone out again. At nightclubs we danced and drank together! On the street or in a club or restaurant we would sometimes hold hands or put our arms around each other. And yet, there was never a violation of trust when it came to our different sexual orientations. I always felt it would have been an insult to act otherwise.

After about two weeks of immensely enjoying each other's company, it came up in conversation that Angie, a lesbian, had *never* been to a strip club! I felt honored to be the one who would take her to see her first female strippers. After all, we could both relate to a sexual attraction to women. I took her to one of the classier strip clubs I had been to several times. I knew the girls at that club were cute and had great bodies. No skanks!

As a tall, attractive young female, Angie always carried herself with great confidence. When she walked into a bar, restaurant, or any place she walked in with the attitude that others noticed her—and they did! But that first night in a strip club revealed a completely different side of her. After we walked into the club and Angie got an immediate sense of what it felt like to be in a strip club, she suggested we sit at the front bar, which was away from the dancing areas.

I asked Angie to pick out a stripper she liked and we would go sit at her stage. So after two drinks she was ready. I had a large stack of dollar bills. Most guys in strip clubs put one dollar on the stage in front of where they are sitting as a signal for the stripper to come over and dance. I was putting three or four dollars in front of Angie. Do I even need to tell you how much attention she got?

Girls who dance in clubs love to dance for other girls. That doesn't mean that all strippers are lesbians, but how could any one who does that for a living have any respect for men? A great number of strippers are, at least, bi-sexual.

Strippers love to dance for women because women, straight or gay, do not project the predatory attitude that men do. I also know that all strippers enjoy attracting attention by catering to the male fantasy of watching two women together.

After Angie had watched a few dances up close at the stage, I told her to pick out a stripper she thought was really "hot" and I would send her upstairs for a "personal dance." Upstairs was where the girls would take *everything* off and strip right in your face, literally! Angie seemed to like one of the strippers more than the others. The stripper had a girlish look. Her hair was in pigtails; she had small, natural breasts and was not plastered with make-up like most strippers.

The stripper got excited as soon as I asked her if she would take my "friend" upstairs for a dance. A private dance upstairs at the club cost $30.00. I gave the girl $45.00 and let her know that Angie was a lesbian and this was her *first* night in a strip club. A smile beamed across the stripper's face! She asked if I wanted to come upstairs and watch her dance for Angie! That's what most men buying a "private dance" for woman wanted to do. They like to *watch*! But this stripper was talking about me watching my new lesbian friend get an up-close and very personal dance. I can honestly say that the thought of watching Angie and the stripper *never* crossed my mind. At this point, some of you must be wondering if I *really* am straight! Well, I am! Even if Angie had wanted me to watch, and I know she didn't, I still would not have gone "upstairs." That would have introduced an aspect of sex into our relationship.

I remember the great satisfaction I felt as I watched the stripper lead Angie upstairs by the hand. Several other strippers had led men upstairs after Angie and her stripper had disappeared; and those girls returned with their clients long *before* Angie did. That led me to believe this stripper was giving Angie my money's worth!

Finally, they came back downstairs to the main part of the club and sat down at a table with me. The stripper seemed to want to spend more time with Angie but she had to get back to dancing for the circles of masculine lust that encompassed each stage. Well, that's not exactly how the stripper put it!

Once alone again I leaned over and asked Angie if she enjoyed it. She formed her hands into a triangular shape, held them right up against her face and said, *"It was right here!!!"* Meaning, of course, that Angie was up close with that special part of stripper's anatomy. Okay, that was enough info for me!

Our adventure to the strip club was on a Wednesday night and I was leaving for Puerto Vallarta that Saturday. I was returning the day after she was leaving with her girlfriend for a trip to Los Angeles. It occurred simultaneously to both of us that we wouldn't be seeing each other for the next two weeks! With a slight pout on her face she said, *"I'm going to miss you!"* And that was exactly the way I felt. That's when I first realized that Angie and I had developed a unique kind of love for each other. I knew it was special and that few people ever experience that sensation.

After checking into the best hotel on the beach in Puerto Vallarta with my girlfriend, Brenda, rather than join her at the poolside bar, I first wanted to hear Angie's voice. My cell phone was useless in

Mexico so I purchased a Mexican phone card. After many frustrating attempts to find a pay phone on the streets of Puerto Vallarta that actually worked, I finally heard Angie's voice! And she sounded as excited to hear mine. It was as if we were two high school sweethearts separated by a family vacation.

I went through several phone cards talking to Angie during my time in Mexico. By the way, my feelings for Angie and my interest in talking to her were no reflection on my wonderful relationship with my girlfriend, Brenda. Looking back, it's a wonder we didn't get arrested in Mexico! Brenda lived in Portland, OR at the time. She returned to Portland and I returned to Denver.

It was two weeks before Angie and I saw each other again. We went out the first night she returned to Denver from her L.A. trip. For the next two weeks we talked several times *every* day. By this time, she began every phone conversation with *"Hi honey"* or *"Hey sweetheart!"* and we both ended by exchanging an *"I love you."* But it was still a friendship between a straight guy with a girlfriend and a lesbian and with a girlfriend.

Angie had been having serious problems with her "controlling" girlfriend and she called me one night to ask if she could spend the night at my apartment because she didn't want her girlfriend to know where she was. She told me that she had friends she could have called, but I was the only one she could trust to really listen to her. She came over with an overnight bag. We talked, she cried, and we talked and she cried. We had become a real-life version of Will & Grace, except in our case the guy was straight and the girl was gay.

Since Angie and I had grown much closer by this point, I wanted to make sure that she didn't think my perception of our relationship had changed. So I invited her to sleep in my bed and while I slept on the sofa. She had an emotionally rough night and in my desire to make her feel secure I pulled the covers up to her neck, said *"Good night,"* and kissed her forehead. Her eyes closed and she smiled. Wait a minute, isn't that the stuff "couples" do!

Angie went to work the next morning and when I got in my shower I noticed that she had left her toothbrush on the ledge. My first thought was that she knew she would be back soon to spend another night. Or, had we grown so close that she would feel closer to me by leaving something of hers behind?

One morning I called Angie like always, but this time there was no answer and no return phone call. She always returned my calls. I called again that afternoon. Still no response. I thought she might have been busy or preoccupied and didn't have time to return the call. The next day was the same. My close lesbian friend would not call back. I had no idea why?

One day I left a message that I was sure would yield a response. The message was, *"I used to have this great lesbian friend, but I don't know what happened to her."* No response. I was hurt. I felt I had lost something special but had no idea why. Several days of not hearing from Angie turned into several weeks.

Angie's absence in my life became a reality. One night out with our cross-dressing friends, Markie and Raven, who introduced Angie to me, Raven noticed I seemed preoccupied and asked me if anything was wrong. I told "her" that I had lost my friendship with Angie and had no idea what had happened. Angie had confided in Raven, who she had known for a long time. Angie said that she was afraid we were getting *too* close and she wanted to end all contact with me. She was concerned that I might be falling in love with her.

Angie had a past experience with a straight guy who was a friend, but fell in love with her and tried to turn their friendship into a real love/sexual relationship. But I had never done *anything* that would have led her to believe I was interested in changing our relationship. She was right. I did *love* her, but it was a unique kind of love that I knew not many have experienced.

From the moment we met, Angie and I instinctively seemed to bond. Yet we were perfect opposites. But what if our relationship had been between Angie, a straight male and me a lesbian? We both confessed that if she were a straight male she would want to be like me and if I were a lesbian I would want to be like her. Perhaps without realizing it consciously, both of us did feel something deeper towards each other. Maybe we had gotten too close.

One night Angie said that she wanted me to go with her and some of her friends on December 7th to celebrate her birthday. I didn't say anything right away. I just thought about how our instant chemistry now made sense. *My* birthday is December 7th!

About two months had passed and I had accepted the reality that my relationship with Angie was history. And then one day she called me! She said she was sorry for the way things ended between us. She went on to say that her controlling girlfriend, the one she was having problems with, had given her an ultimatum: either you stop seeing me or they were through as a couple. Angie expressed regret for allowing her now *ex*-girlfriend to keep us apart. I accepted her regret and the reason she gave for not calling for a couple of months. But was there more to what happened?

Thinking back on how we felt about each other before she stopped calling, I began to realize that we might have gotten too close too quickly. Even though there was respect for each other's sexual orientation, maybe we were beginning to feel something we could no longer explain. Did we begin to feel that our relationship had become so deep that it could defy all that we knew about each other-and ourselves? Individuals are defined by their actions. To act in a way that defies the deepest understanding and expectation we have of ourselves is to change the fundamental trust and beliefs we have in ourselves. We all have an instinct to live within the boundaries that define who we are.

While I was hurt by our "break up," it might have been for the best. Maybe Angie's girlfriend really did give her an ultimatum, or maybe we both became a little scared of what we were beginning to mean to each other. Or maybe it was a little of both.

Angie and I are good friends again. If a week goes by without talking or going out, our next conversation always includes, *"I miss you!"* or *"When am I going to see you?"* But when a period of time goes by without seeing each other we both know the other one is still there and still cares. But it isn't quite the same as it was…maybe one day it will be, or maybe our relationship took the course of any relationship that begins with encompassing infatuation. That early surge of infatuation always fades. Unfortunately.

By the way, the interesting relationship we have is enhanced by our ages-Angie is 27 and I am 53!

My relationship with a lesbian did prove that two people who were destined to never to be a couple could fall in love. If a *straight guy* and a *lesbian* could love each other, then why couldn't a *straight guy* and a *gay guy* or a *straight woman* and a *lesbian* or a *straight woman* and a *gay guy* find the love Angie and I found in each other?

There are benefits to a close relationship between two people with opposite sexual orientations. It's hard to describe, but it's a relationship with someone you can talk to from the same sexual perspective, yet the other person is biologically a girl, or a boy, depending.

There is love beyond the love we feel for family, a spouse, boyfriend, or girlfriend. There is the love I feel for my lesbian friend Angie. I hope you discover *that* love. I hope you find an "Angie!"

The end of the rainbow....

There is a pot of gold at the end of every rainbow...or so the goes *myth*. We can clearly see where the beauty of the rainbow begins and ends but we can never find the pot of gold. As you come to the end of this book I hope you will find the pot of gold that awaits you.

In the months of writing *Get Over the Rainbow*, so much happened that it was impossible to capture and update every development in the continuing battle over gay marriage. In some cases, I had written about a development *before* it actually happened. It was frustrating, but it confirmed that I was on target.

There was the sudden backlash of straight America following the U.S. Supreme Court ruling in the summer of 2003, which declared that gay sex was protected by the Constitution. Then further reaction to the Massachusetts State Supreme Court ruling, which declared there was no wording in the state constitution prohibiting same-sex couples from legal marriage. But as I wrote earlier in the book, the backlash from straight America would subside. Public opinion polls confirmed that the shift in attitudes towards gay marriage had begun even before the 2004 presidential election.

In mid-December 2003, only 31 percent of the adults in America approved of same-sex marriage. That number was down significantly from the previous year. On May 18, 2004, a *USA Today*/CNN/Gallup Poll showed that support for same-sex marriage had grown slightly to 32 percent in February 2004 and to 33 percent by March 2004.

About two weeks before gay and lesbian couples were allowed to marry legally in the state of Massachusetts, the same poll showed support for same-sex marriage in America had risen to 42 percent! The backlash did weaken and that trend will only increase in the next few years.

The issue of gay marriage is following the path of the abortion issue. When the realization sets in that a constitutional amendment banning gay marriage in America amounts to the government controlling a personal decision, support for gay marriage will increase like opposition to abortion decreased. The Republican Party, even with pressure from the Religious Right, will soon loose gay marriage as a conservative social issue.

Throughout this book there were times I digressed. There were reasons for the digressions. Understanding the forces that shape the news daily, the way marketing principles govern controversial issues, and how one need not be homosexual in order to feel a strong bond with the homosexual community, were all crucial to truly understanding the dynamics of the gay marriage debate in America. I also set the record straight for those who fear the influence of Rush Limbaugh and right-wing talk radio. And I enjoyed writing about falling in love with a lesbian and why every heterosexual should have a close homosexual friend.

The fear factor of change

The changing of any tradition is usually met with strong resistance. We are embedded in such a fast-paced, high-tech world that the tendency to cling to a tradition, like marriage, is powerful. Legal gay marriage would change one of civilization's longest standing traditions. Opposition to gay marriage is defined by political and religious beliefs, but the fear of changing a tradition thousands of years old is also part of the resistance. There is a subconscious fear of change, itself, which is independent of the other reasons for opposing gay marriage.

In 1920, there was a debate over whether women should have the right to vote. In the late '50s and into the '60s, black and many white Americans, protested and fought for equal rights for blacks. Laws banning marriages between blacks and whites remained in place after the Civil Rights Act of 1964 was passed.

By the mid-'70s the Women's Liberation Movement encouraged women to burn their bras as a symbol of freedom from a male-controlled society. That was the beginning of women gaining greater status in the workplace and in society. In the '80s, two sides clashed over the controversy of whether Van Halen was better with David Lee Roth or with Sammy Haggar!!!

The '90s brought us the first serious anti-establishment movement since the '60s; and ironically, many young people who fueled the movement with alternative music and grunge fashion were the children of the original anti-establishment generation from the '60s.

The annual controversy over whether homosexuals should be allowed to march in New York's famous St. Patrick's Day Parade exposes one of the fundamental aspects of the gay rights debate. In the parade in New York, the marchers who are gay are seen as gay *first* and Irish *second*. In America, sexual orientation is more important than nationality. On St. Patrick's Day in Ireland, *everyone* is Irish first and gay, lesbian, or whatever second. Nationality should hold more significance than private sex when it comes to judging the merits and value of an individual.

Throughout this book there has been a reminder that the only thing truly separating heterosexuals from homosexuals is the most private act humans engage in: sex. Why should the most private human act become such a divisive issue?

In America, we want everything to be the way *we* think it should be. It is that controlling, egotistical attitude that causes us to expect others to accept homosexuality, reject homosexuality, accept Jesus Christ, reject those who don't accept Jesus Christ, be understanding of the homeless, kick the homeless off the streets, condemn Republicans as intolerant, condemn Democrats as being too tolerant. For reasons discussed earlier in this book individuals now seek specific groups to join in order to find a well-defined identity.

Too many Americans have become lost in a world so homogenized that cultural identity has become difficult to maintain. The protesting and debating over national issues is often the result of individuals crying out to have their voice heard. So they find a cause: maybe it's to protect the Second Amendment, oppose abortion, condemn homosexuality, ban smoking everywhere, or protest the Wal-Mart that will replace small businesses in a neighborhood. As strongly as I denounce anyone who condemns homosexuality, I do pity those who take up causes as a way of finding meaning in their lives.

There is historical precedent which suggests that we will soon look back on this battle over gay rights and gay marriage in the same way we now reflect back on the fight for women's rights, the fight to legalize the use birth control pills, the continuing battle over legal abortion, and the battle for equal rights for blacks. Every one of those issues was met with a divisive battle between two sides that—for the most part—have come together and now realize how wrong it was for a divided America to battle over discrimination based on apparent differences or biological ones.

For the **heterosexuals** who read this book, I hope you will reflect on the historical facts and analogies presented and come to the understanding that the battle for total equality for gays and lesbians in America parallels many battles that have already been fought on the political and social battlegrounds of America.

If you are a heterosexual, the pot of gold you find at the end of this rainbow is the challenge to understand that individuals have the right to lead lives that are congruent with *their* inner compass-not yours. And since a **straight guy** made the arguments supporting gay rights and gay marriage there can be no criticism of this book being written by a homosexual who would personally benefit from the advancement of a gay agenda.

For the **homosexuals** who read this book, I hope you gained more ammunition with which to fight for the rights you deserve, even in the face of those who use their religious beliefs to condemn you in the name of the God who created you.

If you are a homosexual, I hope that your pot of gold at the end of this rainbow is the comfort of knowing that a straight American had the passion and conviction to become a soldier in *your* battle. But as a heterosexual American, I do have something personally to gain from homosexuals winning the right to marriage and all rights offered other Americans. What I gain is what we all gain-the privilege of living in a nation that is fair to *all* individuals.

About the Author

As a successful radio talk show host in New Orleans, Miami, Philadelphia, Seattle and Denver, **Scott Redmond** has become extremely passionate about the debate over gay rights and gay marriage. Redmond has appeared on CNN, MSNBC and the Fox New Channel. He predicted on his radio show in 2000 that the civil rights battle over gay rights would become a major social issue in this decade. He was right.

Currently co-hosting the afternoon talk show on KHOW in Denver, Co., Scott Redmond continues to effectively fight for gay rights. Redmond writes a column for the gay publication. But what makes his new book, **<u>Get Over the Rainbow: why _everyone_ should fight for gay rights</u>** so unique and compelling is….Scott Redmond is **straight!**

www.ingramcontent.com/pod-product-compliance
Lightning Source LLC
Chambersburg PA
CBHW030318290526
45785CB00001B/417